ROLLS-ROYCE

The Author
L J K Setright
L J K Setright is the author of a
number of books on motoring,
motorcycling and aviation. He is
now a consultant in mechanical
and rubber engineering, after a
false start as a lawyer, a profes-
sion he abandoned, deriving
greater satisfaction from writing
The Grand Prix Car, 1954-1966,
Twistgrip, and *The Power to Fly*

Editorial Team

Editor-in-Chief, Ballantine Illustrated History Books
Barrie Pitt

Editorial Director
David Mason

Art Director
Sarah Kingham

Consultant Editor
Prince Marshall

Cover Design : Michael Fry/Graham Bingham
Design : David A Evans

Contents

Photographs and illustrations for this book have been selected from the following archives: Paul Popper Ltd, Montagu Motor Museum, Rolls-Royce Ltd, Ronald Barker, Old Motor Magazine, Park Ward Coachwork, Product Support (Graphics) Ltd, Peter North

At heart a Rolls-Royce man

How does one summarise an international institution within the compass of forty thousand-odd words ?

The story of Rolls-Royce somehow epitomises the whole evolution of mechanised transport in the present century. The cars have always been for the favoured few, even if they are justly rated as economic buys for the high-mileage motorist, but the name is also encountered in the other elements, so much so that the company's vicarious clientele extends far beyond the highways of the world. Piston aero-motors proven in two world wars have given way to gas turbines that power the world's airliners; the Merlin alone has been successfully applied to tanks and power boats as well as aircraft; and Rolls-Royce's latter-day diesels have found new uses in railway locomotives, heavy trucks and construction equipment. Wherever it is found, the name remains a hallmark of supreme quality, in the same way that Sir Alec Issigonis's front-wheel drive masterpiece now epitomises compactness in all countries where English is spoken.

Understandably the saga of Rolls-Royce, from Royce's humble factory in Manchester to the heavily-publicised catastrophe that threatened to engulf the whole enterprise in 1971, is an oft-told story. There have been countless books, monographs and learned articles on the firm's products and the personalities behind them, ranging in scope from unreadable scholarship to tendentious nonsense. Sometimes special pleading has reared its head : for every fanatic for whom anything that Derby or Crewe decrees is right, there is also a would-be debunker only too ready to slate either Rolls-Royce's conservatism (why must the stylists retain that antedeluvian dummy radiator ?) or their concessions to modernity (there is no excuse for standardising an *American* automatic gearbox when one already has the sweetest manual box in the world). In fact the flatterers do more harm than the detractors, for hero-worship is a perilous cult. Most of our worst disappointments come because we expect too much.

Mr Setright has avoided every trap laid for the chronicler. He combines two rare skills – technical erudition and a command of lucid

English – in a fashion which reminds one of the late Laurence Pomeroy, and his criticism is constructive rather than destructive. Further he balances his text evenly between cars and the other elements, between personalities and achievements, between legend and fact. One gains the impression that here we have a reappraisal of Rolls-Royce from Square One, and not just a competent season's gardening in a plot dug, planned, and planted by others.

Further, he has tackled a subject very close to me. I am at heart a Rolls-Royce man, and it would be true to say that I have Spirits of Ecstasy in my blood. My father, as a pioneer motorist, was an early customer of Rolls-Royce, and was chosen to perform the opening ceremony at the Derby works in 1908. Once the Silver Ghost was a fait accompli, he never went back on his loyalty to the marque. Indeed in 1921 he responded to the blandishments of a rival manufacturer (who was, incidentally, a close personal friend as well as a near neighbour at Beaulieu) by observing that 'as a Rolls-Royce man, I would consider it an act of traitorism to take any other car'. Nor did he deviate from this course: at the time of his death in 1929 he was running a Phantom I tourer which I have been fortunate enough to discover and repurchase. It was also my father who inspired the idea of the Spirit of Ecstasy, which was designed by Charles Sykes, who worked for my father's magazine *The Car Illustrated*. Many years later I had the pleasure and privilege of writing the first biography of The Hon Charles Rolls.

I feel it is apposite that this biography should appear at a moment of crisis in the affairs of 'The Best Car in The World'. It is reassuring to know, however, that here is one subject in the present series that is unlikely to join the ranks of the now all-too-fashionable Lost Causes of Motoring.

Lord Montagu of Beaulieu

LIFE BEGINS AT FORTY

'The most conservative genius', concludes Peter Dodds in his study of the orchestration of Brahms, 'will eventually provide more innovation than the most revolutionary talent.'

It is a fascinating hypothesis: it provides a fresh basis for examining the lives of many famous men, from Moses or Leonardo da Vinci to Ghandi or Ricardo. In the case of Henry Royce, it provides a perfect defence to the allegation often levelled at him that he was a mere improver incapable of original creative design. Really one has only to examine his innovations in electrical machinery to see that such allegations are easily refuted; but if we limit ourselves to the study of his cars and aero engines we may still find ample evidence to qualify him as that particular kind of conservative genius. After all, what kind of innovation might reasonably have been expected of him? Have we any right to demand a stressed-skin Silver Ghost, or a compound turbocharged Kestrel? Of course not; but, say his detractors, far from

being years ahead of his contemporaries he always lagged behind them, merely adapting and perhaps perfecting what others had conceived and proved. This surely is where the conservatism may be identified: Royce was always prepared to work out his own original solution to a given problem, but only after he had satisfied himself that no potential solution might be found in the inchoate works of others. Is it reasonable to expect that he should deliberately turn a blind eye to the products of other intelligent brains, and waste precious time in arriving independently at what might turn out to be the same end?

As for the genius, how shall we identify that? I do not subscribe to the hackneyed definition of genius as so many percent inspiration and so many more of perspiration, otherwise there would be no merit in labour and the car would never have replaced the horse, nor even the cavalier have defeated the infantryman. To my mind, the essential prerequisite to genius is curiosity, the compulsive perception of imperfection. It was this quality in Royce which made his name famous all around the world; by seeing how much better certain things could be done, and by being able to do them accordingly.

For what other innovation should we look? His exquisite electrical ancillaries? His highly refined carburettors? His delicately wrought governors? No, these are mere baubles. Royce's outstanding contribution to automotive engineering was his revaluation of quality. Before his time, quality was something vague that might be assessed by considering surface finish, decoration and kindred meretricious things; but Royce identified quality with mechanical integrity, in the process giving us cars whose unimpeachable manners and legendary reliability allowed us to judge such machines by new standards.

It is hard to see where he could have acquired his own standards. His childhood was impoverished, his youth hard, his whole life so consumed with work that he had little time for social intercourse. He seems instead to have had an intuitive appreciation of what was good, backed up by the facility for logical examination of whatever might be dubious.

In a world such as ours, even such a world as was his at the turn of the century, such gifts alone are not enough to ensure survival in the world of commerce. Fortunately Royce was blessed with colleagues who were well able to supply his deficiencies. There was the secretary De Looze who looked after administration at Rolls-Royce until the 1940s; there was the Hon C S Rolls, who helped Royce gain fame at the beginning of his motor manufacturing career; and most important of all, there was Claude Johnson, a brilliant businessman whose flair for promoting the company's products was equalled only by the commercial acumen with which he planned the company's future policy.

Royce was forty years old when in 1903 he began to take an interest in motor cars. At that time Johnson was just on the point of resigning the secretaryship of what we now know as the Royal Automobile Club in order to apply his administrative gifts to the promotion of the business of C S Rolls and Co, of which he was partner and joint managing director. The Hon Charles Stewart Rolls had for some time been running this motor business, having several agencies of which the most distinguished had originally been that of Panhard; but this French make was losing its erstwhile supremacy, and Rolls was anxious to find a good British car to replace it. In fact he was more ambitious than that: for he confided to a friend that his aim was to have his name associated with a car so good that the name would be universally associated with all that was best in motoring, enjoying a fame in that field such as that enjoyed by the name Steinway among pianos.

Royce was simply concerned with making a good car. In 1902 he had bought his first, a Decauville, but from the very beginning it was unsatisfactory. When he went to the goods station at London Road Manchester to collect it, the car simply would not start despite all his efforts, and he was obliged to hire four men to push it through the streets to the factory in Cooke Street where F H Royce and Co Ltd had a now flourishing business as makers of electric cranes and dynamos. Royce was chief engineer there, and the contributions he had made in the past to the state of the art of designing and manufacturing electrical machinery, dynamos in particular, give the lie to any idea that he was incapable of original work. It was his engineering skills, combined with the business skills of his partner Claremont, that had raised the firm from the level of a backyard workshop making eighteen-penny domestic bell sets to the status of a company with an international reputation, even enjoying the tribute of having its cranes copied faithfully by the Japanese.

Now in 1902 Royce began to take an

9

The chassis of the first Royce car, the 10hp

interest in motoring, and he was shocked by the engineering solecisms that he identified in contemporary cars, including his own Decauville. That insatiable curiosity set him to work analysing the problems of motor car design, and before long he had concluded that he should make some cars himself. The electrical and crane business was entering a slight decline, and with the bulk of the crane motor and foundry work having been transferred to another factory at Trafford Park, there was some spare capacity in the old Cooke Street premises where Royce fancied he could build three experimental cars which might serve as prototypes for a production model.

Claremont was not at all keen. Somehow Royce managed to persuade the others that he should proceed with his idea, and after a lot of thinking and tinkering, adapting the Decauville design where it seemed good and super-

vising his own improvements where it seemed otherwise (notably in the electrics, the carburettor and gearbox where Royce devised a freewheel to simplify the task of gearchanging) and after long hours of bench running and careful development work, the first 10hp two-cylinder Royce car was completed and made a trial run on the 1st April 1904.

This first car and its two stable-mates were eminently successful, being far more flexible, quiet, reliable and refined than their contemporaries. Before long, the qualities of the Royce car were to enjoy widespread publicity, journalists of the day (notably Massac Buist) being quite enthusiastic about this apparently simple but inimitably refined little car. Already, however, the news of Royce's work had been passed by Claremont to a man named Edmunds with whom he was doing a deal in shares in Royce Ltd and W T Glover and Co, a cable-making firm. Edmunds passed the information on to Rolls and, having written to him a letter of recommendation, then sought the cooperation of Royce in arranging a meeting between the two men. Royce was too busy to be interested, but eventually Mohammed came to the mountain.

The outcome of Roll's visit to Manchester was that his company agreed to take all the cars made by Royce; soon after, it was further agreed that they should be called Rolls-Royces. In 1906 came the formation of Rolls-Royce Ltd – and here our story will really start.

By the time that the Royce car had become the Rolls-Royce, progress was well in hand with ideas that Royce had nurtured for some time for versions of his car with three, four and even six cylinders. Rolls was enthusiastic, knowing that the quality in England and elsewhere were more concerned with refinement of running than anything else, and realising that such a multiplicity of cylinders must lead to a car of exceptional merit if the basic two-cylinder Royce was any indication. He also knew that no amount of good engineering would compensate, as far as the customer was concerned, for any shortcomings in external appearances, and he and Johnson impressed upon Royce that a good deal more spit and polish was necessary. By the time of the Paris Show at the end of 1905, all except the six-cylinder 30hp cars were ready. This was the result of really frenzied work at Cooke Street, some of which went into the making of a dummy engine for the 20hp car. Such mock-ups are not uncommon at motor shows, and the public were not likely to notice, being seduced instead by the beautiful finish of the cars and the superb appearance of the new Palladian radiator.

Royce is supposed to have modelled

Rolls about to take the Duke of Connaught for a drive in the original 2-cylinder Royce

Lillie Hall – a former roller-skating rink acquired by C S Rolls in 1902. Used by Rolls-Royce as a chassis distribution centre. In the background is a bus chassis imported from Italy which Rolls was hopeful of marketing under the Rolls name

First 15hp. Rolls-Royce Landaulette exhibited at Paris Salon, 1904.

The first of three 15hp 3-cylinder cars built by Royce, shown as a Rolls-Royce at the 1904 Paris Salon

this on the radiator of the defunct Norfolk car, which went out of production in 1903; but the most important feature of the radiator, the application of the principle of entasis (by which the ancient Greek architects overcame the distortion produced naturally by the human eye, by introducing a slight convexity to 'flat' surfaces) must be credited to Royce himself. More to the point, only Royce was enough of a perfectionist to insist upon the radiator being fashioned in accordance with this principle despite the formidable manipulative problems that it created in manufacture. Hindsight shows that he was right to insist; and when in later years he wanted to change the shape of the radiator because it now seemed to him to offend against all established aerodynamic tenets, Johnson was equally adamant that a Rolls-Royce

without that radiator was no Rolls-Royce, and that it should not under any circumstances be abandoned.

Of the new engines which resided behind this imposing facade the three-cylinder had the shortest production life. Only six examples were made. There was nothing wrong with them; after all, an in-line three has none of the vibrational problems of a twin or four, and need not be beset by problems of torsional vibration in the crankshaft as in the in-line six; only a conical couple requires to be constrained, which is easy. The short life of the 15hp three-cylinder Rolls-Royce was simply due to the fact that it did not fit into the rationalised production scheme in which cylinder blocks were cast for pairs of cylinders – one of which set the two-cylinder car on its way, two producing the 20hp four-cylinder engine, and three of which might make the 30hp six. The three-cylinder engine had to have separate

The Hon Charles Stewart Rolls

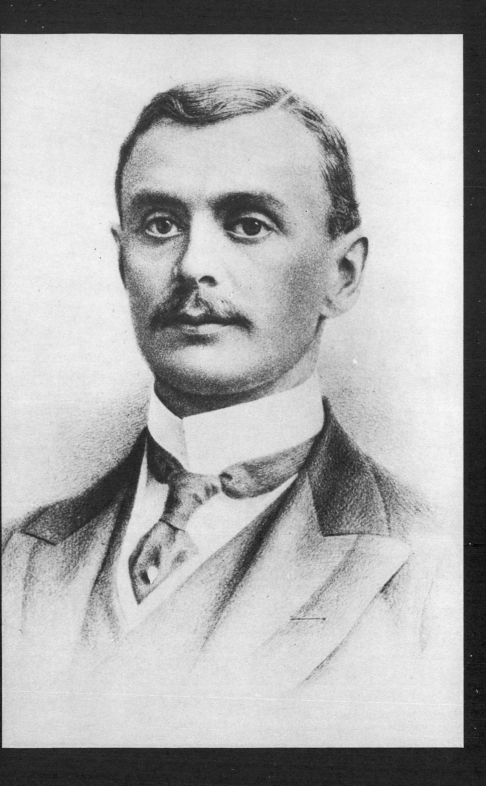

At the 1906 motor show the
Rolls-Royce name appeared before
the public still under the shadow of
C S Rolls

Above: Cooke Street, Manchester, where Royce had his first factory
Below: Early Rolls-Royce cars being assembled at Cooke Street

cylinders, or else be redesigned – and rather than embark on this and on development of the crankshaft, which needed more careful balancing than anybody at the time had the skill to give it, the model was abandoned.

The 20hp four-cylinder Rolls-Royce was an immediate success, enjoying the acclaim of all who drove it. Rolls could sell all that Royce could make – and he made forty in the course of 1905 and 1906. However, Rolls knew the value of publicity, knew that competition success (especially in racing) was a particularly convincing form of advertisement, and had plenty of experience in racing to give him confidence in entering a Rolls-Royce in the Tourist Trophy that was to be held in the Isle of Man in September 1905. Accordingly he persuaded Royce to prepare two specially modified four-cylinder cars for this event.

The TT was nothing like the stampede of giants that the typical road race of the day resembled, being designed to encourage the improvement of the ordinary touring car; and not only in performance but also in economy, reliability and sundry other respects. Full four- or five-seater touring bodies had to be fitted, and the car had to be ballasted to the equivalent of four adult passengers, though only the driver and mechanic would ride in the race. There was a strict weight limit and a secretly prepared fuel consumption handicap, but these constraints gave Royce little or no difficulty. He had already introduced nickel steels for his chassis and axles, and the greater strength: weight ratio of these materials made it possible to build the cars considerably lighter than could be achieved with the ordinary mild steel commonly used by other manufacturers. Weight was therefore not a problem; as for fuel consumption, the advanced design of Rolls-Royce carburettors and the low mechanical losses consequent on careful manufacture and assembly made the car naturally frugal, but Royce developed it further with the substitution of a new four-speed gearbox for the earlier three-speed one, direct drive remaining on third gear with fourth a geared-up overdrive intended only to give more economical running at speed.

One way and another, the Tourist Trophy Rolls-Royce was a superb car. Before the practice sessions began in the Isle of Man during the week preceding the race day, most experts dismissed it as unlikely to have the performance necessary to succeed in the event, the silence and docility of the Rolls-Royce giving no hint of any pretensions to speed. They changed their tune somewhat when Rolls covered a practice lap of the 52-mile road circuit at an average speed of 33mph and doing 26mpg withal, on a route that was generally rough and notoriously hilly. When the organisers announced that the permitted fuel consumption would be 22.54mpg, confidence in the ability of the Rolls-Royce to do well was greatly reinforced.

These hopes were rudely shattered in the very first lap of the race. Rolls, his excitement getting the better of his driving technique, wrecked the gearbox of his car before it had travelled a mile. This left Northey as the sole representative of Rolls-Royce hopes, but he was certainly doing well. Indeed on his third lap he did the fastest of the day, and in the end he finished second to an Arrol-Johnston by the satisfactorily small margin of 0.2mph. Of course it was considered a pity that Northey could not have won; but, bearing in mind the fact that the Rolls-Royce was a new and almost unknown make this qualified success really did its reputation a lot of good. Johnson, who hitherto had not been inclined to give the Rolls-Royce too much attention (which would have been at the expense of the other cars for which the Rolls firm retained agencies) now devoted himself with a will to the R-R and the car justified his confidence with a convincing win in the TT, while Johnson went campaigning with the 30hp car in the arduous Scottish Reliability Trials. A number of other competitions were also entered with

Above: In 1906 the 20hp Rolls-Royce won the TT, and this is the car
(with Rolls at the wheel and Johnson beside him) which, according to
contemporary publicity, did it
Below: Northey at the wheel of the 20hp Rolls-Royce in which he finished
second in the 1905 Tourist Trophy. Sitting behind him is Rolls

Above: The actual TT car, prepared with such care to suit the stringent regulations governing the event, was distinguished by copious lightening holes in the chassis frame and hubs, and by wire-spoked wheels
Below: To prove this is the car – a picture taken during the actual race

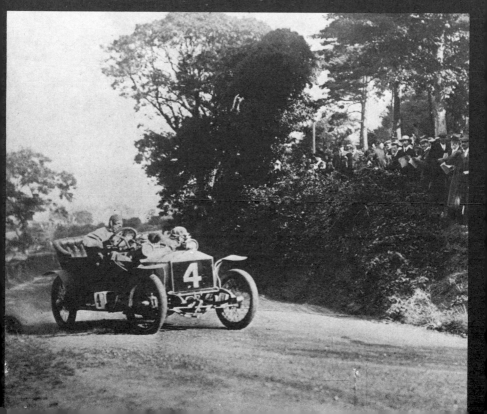

The Legalimit, a V8–engined folly which acted as custodian of the driver's conscience, being governed to a maximum speed of 20mph

reasonable success, not only in Britain and Europe but also in America, where Rolls made a good impression with one of the four-cylinder cars.

In the circumstances it might have been expected that Rolls-Royce would have proceeded with the promotion and development of their existing cars. For some reason, however, Johnson took it into his head that Royce should design a luxury town car whose engine was to be so self-effacing that it could neither be seen, felt, heard nor smelt. In effect it was to be an old fashioned town carriage without a horse, a bonnetless monument to self-propelled antiquarianism. Another idea (conjured up by Sir Henry Harmsworth) was that Rolls-Royce should make a car which, beside having all the qualities for which the make was already renowned, should be self-governing in such a way that it would be impossible for its driver to be guilty of exceeding the legal limit of speed, which was then 20mph. Royce treated these two problems as one and conceived a V8 engine, its cylinder banks set at an included angle of ninety degrees and its crankshaft throws at 180 degrees, the cylinders being cast in groups of two and having bore and stroke of $3\frac{1}{4}$ inches each, the total swept volume coming to just $3\frac{1}{2}$-litres. The two new cars employing this engine did in fact all that was demanded of them, and they were launched in a blaze of publicity.

Perhaps unfortunately, but certainly not surprisingly, they were commercial failures: the horseless carriage looked too absurd for words, and as for the 'Legalimit' as it was called, the public saw no reason why Rolls-Royce should set themselves up as keepers of the customers' consciences.

Suitably chastened, Johnson did his best to promote the 30hp six-cylinder car which was his particular favourite. He had a lot of competition from Napier and others, but the greatest hurdle he had to overcome was a basic short-coming of his own car – the suscepti-bility to crankshaft failure that was due (though it was not generally appreci-ated at the time) to the torsional vibration which is peculiarly trouble-some in six-in-line engines. Royce tried one thing after another to raise the critical speed of the crankshaft (at which the rotational speed of the crank is one-third of the natural fre-quency of the shaft) to a rate that was higher than might be reached in service. By the end of 1905 he had run out of ideas, and decided that future modification would be hopeless. A complete redesign was necessary. Thus was born the 40/50, the car that established the company beyond ques-tion as the makers of the best in the world, the car that Johnson recognised was so good that it and it alone should enjoy the undivided concentration of the factory to the exclusion of all other models, the car that was to enjoy lasting fame and ungrudging honour as the Silver Ghost.

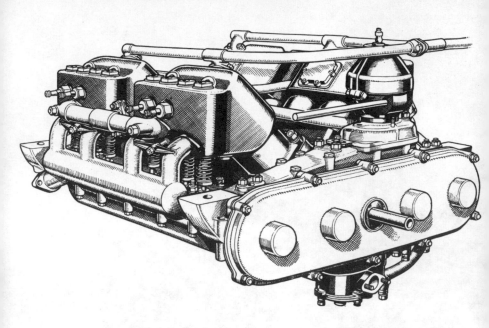

Above: Had Rolls-Royce continued to develop their early vee engines they may have eventually stolen much of Cadillac and Ford glory
Below: The first 30hp 6-cylinder car wore this Pullman limousine body

Above: The 30hp 'six' was supposed to be Johnson's pet, but Rolls is driving this example. He usually stuck to the 4-cylinder models
Below: The 30hp RR taking part in the Scottish Reliability Trials of 1908

THE
MASTERPIECE

The engineering of Royce, the standing of Rolls, and the commercial flair of Johnson, made the company and its early cars well enough known and highly respected. It was the 40/50 model, however, that earned the reputation of being the best car in the world. This is something that no other Rolls-Royce car has ever done: for although it may have been arguable that some of the successors to the Silver Ghost may have been entitled in their turn to be deemed the best car in the world in their respective times, not one of them can really be said to have *earned* the reputation – it simply came ready-made, an inheritance of inestimable value. It is unlikely that any of the later models could really justify the claim that the company and its admirers so doggedly asserted; but in the case of the Silver Ghost the company could boast that it was the world's best car (the accolade was originally bestowed by a journalist) not only with pride but also with good reason.

There may have been nothing superficially outstanding about the design, for Royce as we know was not a deliberately innovative engineer; but there was a wealth of detailed perfection in it bearing witness to the fact that Royce was a gifted mechanic with an uncannily shrewd and perceptive technical (as opposed to scientific) brain; and these detailed felicities of design were backed by a quality control more rigorous perhaps than any that has since been known in the motor car industry, and undoubtedly far more stringent than anything that had been practised before.

Perhaps such standards were more necessary then. Today, only the most lowly and ignorant of tyros would perpetrate the monstrous atrocities of mechanical cruelty or be guilty of the intellectual apathy which characterised the majority of drivers in those far-off days. Impeccable flexibility in top gear was demanded because there were few drivers competent to get out of it once they were in it: gear changing was generally considered an esoteric

art form and there were not man[y] prepared to devote themselves t[o] acquiring the appropriate skills. Relia[-] bility had to be faultless because it wa[s] a rare man who was so well instructe[d] as to be able to perform an effectiv[e] diagnosis of any malady less obviou[s] than that everyday occurrence, [a] punctured tyre. Engine performanc[e] was necessarily mediocre because th[e] metals then available would not stan[d] the extremes of temperature tha[t] reduced even the most beautifull[y] wrought racing engine to scrap in [a] few hundred miles, while the lubr[i-] cants available were either of abysm[al] quality (in the case of the mineral oils[)] or else inconveniently idiosyncrati[c] and socially objectionable. Furthe[r] more, fuel was of dubious quality an[d] greatly varying specification: the pi[o-] neers of motoring simply had to choos[e] between low grade petrol and benzol[e] or, if they could not choose, to combin[e] the two. Geographical consideration[s] affected their choice: the Germans ha[d] moderate supplies of highly aromat[ic] petrol but enjoyed plenty of benzol[e] produced from coal in which they wer[e] rich – as they were in good chemist[s.] The British obtained their petrol fro[m] Rumania and from the Dutch Ea[st] Indies, petrol from the latter sourc[e] being very high in aromatic conte[nt] and (though it was not known at th[at] time) with an anti-knock value of 7[0] octane or higher. The Americans g[ot] along as best as they could with petr[ol] that was seldom up to 50-octane ratin[g] though Californian petrol was a good [a] Dutch East Indian. The result was that [a] car which might be sold anywhere [in] Europe or might have to travel an[y] where across America had to be able [to] operate effectively on almost any bre[w] so its engine had to have a low com[-] pression ratio, be as free as possibl[e] from tendencies to detonation or pr[e-] ignition, and to require the absolu[te] minimum of attention by the driver [to] his ignition advance and retard contr[ol]

One way or another, then, a good ca[r] had to be a gentle car. If it had an[y] pretensions to performance, such pe[r-]

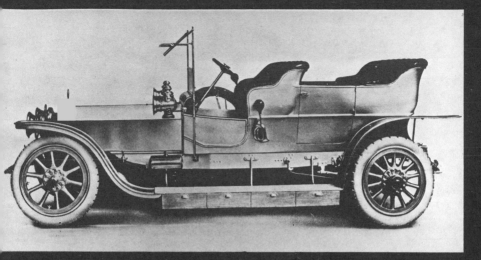

The Silver Ghost, at the start of a golden age, and with half a million miles ahead of it

ormance had to be achieved with the aid of a large engine rather than a notably efficient one. It it had any pretensions to elegance, it would have to be capable of carrying a body that would have been constructed with loving care, considerable skill, and a sublime disregard for the exigencies of motoring on bad roads with coarsely-sprung, flexible and underpowered chassis. That is to say, the body would be excessively heavy, structurally precarious, aerodynamically indefensible, and would make a considerable contribution to the instability of the vehicle upon which it was mounted. It would provide little or no insulation against noise or vibration originating in or transmitted by the chassis (including the engine); and yet the motorist would be guiltily insistent on quietness for a high level of noise of either mechanical or gaseous origin would perhaps frighten a horse – the most heinous social solecism of the time – and surely the occupants of the car were entitled to as much peace and quiet as the horses with which they shared the road. They therefore demanded mechanical silence, or at least reasonable quietness and freedom from the intrusions of gear noise from engine and transmis-

The chassis of the 40/50 RR

Every Silver Ghost chassis was thoroughly tested, and to aid this RR built a private test track in the grounds of their Derby works. This is how one of its superelevated corners looked in 1909

sion, and also a reasonable freedom from vibrations transmitted by the suspension or generated by the engine.

Being perfectly attuned to these demands, the Rolls-Royce 40/50 was assured of success. Its chassis was broadly similar to that of the earlier 30hp car, but the engine which gave it its title was completely new. The 40 was in round terms the horsepower according to the RAC rating, determined according to piston area and thus a product of six cylinders each of $4\frac{1}{2}$-inch bore, disregarding with splendid theoretical assurance the supposed irrelevance of the stroke which was in this case also $4\frac{1}{2}$-inches. The 50 was in

even rounder terms the actual output of the engine in brake horsepower, the product of 7,036cm³ running at a compression ratio of 3.2:1 and a brake mean effective pressure of somewhat less than 70 lb/in².

Unlike the earlier six-cylinder engine, that of the 40/50 appears as a brace of threes in line, rather than as three twins: externally this could be seen from the two cast iron cylinder blocks with their integral heads, each block perched on the long aluminium alloy crankcase within which the conical couples of two reciprocally arranged three-cylinder engines were mutually self-cancelling, only the extra long centre main bearing testifying to the unequal distribution of loads characteristic of the type. There were altogether seven main bearings for the crankshaft, itself a particularly robust piece of work by the standards of its time although devoid of balance weights. In fact the

main journals and the crank pins were nearly twice as thick as those of the 30hp engine, demanding something more positive than the rudimentary lubrication system upon which that earlier specimen relied, and Royce employed instead the pressure feed of oil to the bearings to the hollow crankshaft, as he had done in his V8 engines.

The most obvious feature of the new engine was its side valve layout. When compression ratios were perforce so low, when cam profiles were still artlessly simple, and when cylinder head gaskets were treacherously unreliable, such a layout had everything to commend it – provided that the foundry men were capable of casting one-piece cylinders with sufficient space for water to flow reasonably near to the valve seats. The absence of the pushrods which Royce had hitherto used for operating overhead inlet valves eliminated a potential source of

mechanical noise, which could further be minimised by adjustment of the tappets (not always accepted as necessary by other designers of the period) which, together with the valve springs, were left exposed along the left-hand side of the engine. The timing drive to crankshaft and ignition was by gears, for Royce was utterly opposed to the use of chains anywhere; and only the cooling fan remained to be driven by a link belt from a pulley on the nose of the crankshaft.

It was in its ancillaries that the engine of the 40/50 displayed exceptional merit. As in every other of Royce's cars the electrical apparatus was of outstanding quality, recalling the origins of the company. The distributor, the trembler coils and the high tension magneto were Royce's own, abetted by four-volt accumulators that served the coils, two sparking plugs serving each cylinder. The drill in

those days was to start on the coil and thereafter run on the magneto, so as to avoid draining the accumulator, though the poor performance of a magneto at low rates of revolution made it desirable to keep both ignition systems switched on when travelling slowly in top gear. Later, when fashion and experience decreed that the time was right – that is to say, in 1919 – Royce was to equip the 40/50 with a dynamo so as to maintain the charge of the electrical accumulators for lighting and starting; and thereafter a non-trembler coil surplanted the original component, whereupon it became normal to run with both ignition systems switched on all the time. This did not rob the car of its impressive ability to start on the switch, which any decently kept specimen will do even after standing for several hours. The trembler coil would provide a cascade of sparks sufficient to ignite the mixture remaining in the cylinder, but on later cars it was sufficient to flick the distributor points open and shut by moving the ignition advance control lever. A driver strange to the ways of Royce and sitting at the wheel of a 40/50 for the first time might search in vain for this lever, for nowhere would he see the telltale words *advance* and *retard* which were literally the *lingua franca* of the day: Royce despised what he considered thoughtless adaption of the French language, and substituted the words *early* and *late*. He is known to have been intolerant of people who toyed with foreign tongues, and his readiness with invective gave him no use for what the historian Gibbon once described as 'the decent obscurity of a learned language', so he used to goad his accountant de Looze unmercifully when that hapless servant indulged his fancy for Latin tags. Nevertheless Royce swallowed his objections to the Latin when the company established its

This 1909 chassis carries a landaulette body, opened to show with rare clarity what contemporary standards of headroom were

motto *quiqvis recte factum, quamvis humile, praeclarum:* whatsoever is done aright, however humble, is noble. Be it never so humble, the Rolls-Royce is the best car in the world . . .

One of the things which persuaded the driver of the car's excellence was the sheer tactile pleasure of handling the controls, even the minor ones being fitted with such accuracy as to give them a feel rivalling that of slip gauges or the finest machine tools. Indeed, in the mechanical refinements of its control systems the Rolls-Royce was practically beyond comparison with other cars. The governor system, for example, was widely criticised as being unnecessary and therefore an extravagance; but those who learned to use it appreciated that the complication and expense were an investment bringing a return in pleasure and assurance when driving. Fashioned with great precision and delicacy, the centrifugal governor was interlinked with the accelerator pedal control so as to supplement it but to be overridden by it – and it was therefore quite different from the simple constant-speed governor associated with more primitive engines. If the driver released the accelerator pedal, the engine would immediately adjust its revolutions to coincide with whatever speed had been predetermined by the driver's setting of the governor, be it a tick-over that would do credit to an industrial gas engine or a rate such as would maintain the car's road speed perfectly constant regardless of gradient. Some drivers exploited the governor in order to achieve a silent and smooth gearchange without any need for skilful co-ordination of feet and hands. This trick, taught by Rolls-Royce at their drivers' school, was the secret of the smooth progress achieved by many a chauffeur who seemed incapable of anything demanding a higher level of skills than changing a wheel or leathering the paintwork.

There have been many cars – and some are still made even today – based on the premise that the customer is

Charles Sykes' Silver Fancy provided the inspiration for the RR mascot

Sykes' Spirit of Ecstasy was adopted for RR radiator caps.

Rolls in his Wright biplane at Bournemouth in 1910, just before taking off for the last time

always right, and designed so as to be forgiving of bad driving. There are and have been many more distinguished by an uncompromising inability to suffer fools, cars that are rewarding to the skilled driver but forbidding to those of less accomplishment. The 40/50 was that rarity, a car that forgives the bad driver and rewards the good: while countless customers piled ineptitude upon indifference and submitted the car to gross indignities which it suffered with stoic or even saintly perseverence, several addicts – some of them employees of the company, others private gentleman – made the most of its high performance, good handling and remarkable endurance by taking part with a good measure of success in all sorts of motoring competitions, ranging from the Alpine Trials to record-breaking long distance runs between point A, which might be Monaco for instance, to

point B which might be London. But the very first 40/50 thus to sue for the attention and approbation of the public was submitted to an exhaustive and convincing test by Claude Johnson himself. This was the thirteenth chassis, fitted with silver-painted touring body on which all appropriate metal fittings were silver plated, while on the scuttle gleamed a cast name plate identifying this car as Silver Ghost.

Thus was born that resplendent and revered name, originally to distinguish this particular car but eventually to identify the whole genus of Rolls Royce 40/50 models from 1907 to 1925. Johnson, with his flair for publicity, thus gave the car a persona, if not personality, which helped to attract attention during the trials to which the car was then subjected. First there was a 2,000 miles trial carried out under RAC observation, taking in a drive from Bexhill to Glasgow using only third (direct drive) and fourth (overdrive) gears, as well as a lot of running around plotting the course for the Scottish

Trial with which the RAC were about to concern themselves. The car was then dismantled and checked by an RAC engineer who, prepared like Hotspur to cavil at the ninth part of a hair, could find nothing to criticise but a slight movement of the rings on one piston. After the Silver Ghost was reassembled it participated in the Scottish Trial and thereafter was driven to and fro between London and Glasgow, stopping only on Sundays, until it had completed 15,000 miles and the RAC observers were wondering when their invigilation might ever end. There was only one involuntary stop, quite early in the trial, when a loose petrol tap shook itself into the closed position during the Scottish Trial; but apart from the minute penalty that this incurred, the car ran like clockwork for 14,371 miles. Then it was taken apart again and this time the RAC engineers reported slight wear in some steering parts and a need for repacking the water pump. None of

these conditions was sufficiently serious to demand immediate attention, but Johnson insisted on the worn components being replaced; and when this was done, the bill for parts was seen to be £2 2s 7d.

Here then was the reward of such painstaking construction, and the return on such an expensive investment: running costs were amazingly low, so the Silver Ghost could be considered an economical car to run. During the Trial it had already demonstrated an astonishingly frugal average fuel consumption of 17.8 miles per gallon, while yet being sufficiently blessed with engine to be able to accelerate from $3\frac{1}{2}$ to 53mph in third gear and go on to a top speed of 63mph. Bearing in mind that the gross vehicle weight was less than 50lb short of two tons, this was a

Taking part in a spot landing competition, Rolls crashed his Wright and was killed

remarkable performance; and Johnson saw to it that it enjoyed plenty of publicity. Anticipating an enthusiastic reaction to the news that this supremely elegant, quiet and competent machine could be run at $4\frac{1}{2}$d a mile all in, Rolls-Royce put the Silver Ghost into full production, beginning at the rate of four cars a week. Had they known it, they would probably have felt no surprise in the knowledge that they were to build 6,173 Silver Ghosts in the course of eighteen years, an average (including the years of the Great War) of better than seven per week.

The model did not of course continue unchanged. Within two years some important alterations were made to the specification, the most notorious being a replacement of the four-speed gearbox with its geared-up fourth speed, its place being taken by a normal three-speed affair. This change seemed to Royce entirely logical, for nearly all drivers went everywhere in top gear, and were apparently incapable of assimilating the significance of an overdrive ratio, insisting on treating the highest speed of the four-speed box as though it were a conventional top. Since it was an indirect gear and since even Rolls-Royce mechanics were fallible, this fourth speed could be heard when engaged; and this constituted a lapse from the standards that Royce fought so energetically to maintain. If they wanted to go everywhere in top gear, then the customer should have a top gear that was suitable – and it need not be a low gear, a stratagem to which many other contenders for the luxury car market were not too proud to resort.

In most circumstances the three-speed gearbox was eminently satisfactory, but when it came to starting on a 1 in 4 gradient during the 1912 Austrian Alpine Trial, when the high bottom gear ratio and the high altitude conspired to limit the tractive effort available, one of the competing Silver Ghosts failed to restart until the passengers dismounted. In any other car this might have occasioned a cluck

of the tongue, but for a Rolls-Royce it was a disgraceful episode, and all appropriate steps were taken to redeem the car's reputation. Thus in 1913 a normal four-speed gearbox with direct top replaced the three-speeder, first in the so-called Continental model and later in the standard chassis, and a team of three cars was entered in the 1913 Austrian Alpine Trial, backed by a fourth privately entered by that great driver James Radley. The four Rolls-Royces made mincemeat of the opposition, giving an almost perfect display of that effortless superiority which is the mark of good breeding. They were not perfectly standard – and neither, we must suppose, was any of their rivals; but the differences were more interesting than critical. One feature of the specially prepared cars was that they had aluminium alloy pistons, and they were sprung at the rear by an improved version of the cantilevered half-elliptics that had been produced for the London-to-Edinburgh cars.

The London-to-Edinburgh episode was one which grew out of a challenge issued by Napier in 1911, when that company was being publicised by S F Edge. The contest involved a run from London to Edinburgh in top gear, and subject to RAC supervision, followed by a run at Brooklands and including a fuel consumption test. The 55hp car submitted by Napier did 76.42mph aroud the outer circuit and its fuel consumption was noted at 19.35-mpg. The Rolls-Royce, with tapered bonnet, raised compression and larger carburettor as well as the new cantilever rear suspension, did 78.26mph and 24.32mpg. It was then stripped and fitted with a higher axle ratio and a narrow single-seat racing body, in which trim it was timed at 101.8mph over a quarter mile at Brooklands, driven by Hives.

It was from the London-to-Edinburgh type, a few of which were offered for sale, that the Continental Silver Ghost was developed; and this in turn became the standard model when peace came again after the Great War.

This is the original London–Edinburgh car of 1911, of which so many replicas were made

Considering how many things were so greatly changed by the war, it may seem surprising that Rolls-Royce could have been content to resume production of their pre-war car, and to do so on a scale which suggested that they had every intention of maintaining it for some considerable time. In fact the market was booming, and they could

not satisfy its demands fast enough; to delay matters by evolving a new model, this being an especially time-consuming process when Rolls-Royce development standards were so exhaustive, would mean the loss of many

In its day the London–Edinburgh Silver Ghost was uncommonly handsome, and even when more copiously equipped (like this 1911 replica) its long low profile gave it inimitable style

Ghosts could still be high in 1912, like these in France

valuable sales and (even more important) the loss of a great deal of goodwill. People were ready, anxious and able to buy Silver Ghosts; what could be more natural than that the company should with equal alacrity supply them?

The Rolls-Royce version ran as follows: 'During the War the whole energies of the Rolls-Royce Company were directed towards the production of armoured cars and aero engines in large quantities. The productive capacity of the company's works was greatly increased. Yet there has never been the slightest deviation from the company's traditional policy that superlative quality is the foremost and greatest consideration of all. Since the Armistice, therefore, it is not surprising that the Rolls-Royce chassis has been found to be the only type which could stand the enormous strain of armoured car duties in Mesopotamia and elsewhere. The Rolls-Royce aero engines

also achieved the conquest of the Atlantic and have proved to be the most trustworthy engines for post-war commercial aviation. The post-war period finds the world more than ever convinced that the motor car is one of the essentials of civilised life. The Rolls-Royce post-war car is just as far in advance of the ordinary car as was the pre-war model. It still maintains the lead over all its contemporaries which it acquired fifteen years ago, and it is more true than ever to say that a Rolls-Royce never wears out.'

Some of the claims thus made would be difficult to substantiate; but if we judge them as the publicity material that they are, we need not consider them exorbitant. In fact the Silver Ghost was still made with an expensive disregard for any consideration that might prejudice its quality.

Factory methods are always difficult to evaluate. The ordinary man is no judge of the accuracy or repeatability of a given type of machine tool, though he is right in suspecting that it can vary tremendously according to the materials it is working, the cutting lubricants used, the skill of the setter, the preparation of the cutting tool and so on. The same applies to handwork: any fitter who takes a reasonable pride in his work will assure you that he is one of the only three men in England who know how to use a file properly, but how good might his work be on Monday morning or Saturday afternoon? In the case of the Rolls-Royce factory at Derby however, the things that marked the production of the Silver Ghost as being in a different class to that of any other car were things involving design expertise rather than artisan skills – though the latter could be taken for granted, since Royce visited summary dismissal upon any man he saw mishandling a tool.

For example, forgings were designed so that the grain flow of the finished machined product should be most favourable. In the case of the brake drum this meant that a forging weighing 106lb in its raw state ended up as a beautiful brake drum weighing 32lb. Even more extreme was the connecting rod, finished at 2lb from a forging weighing eight, with only the perfect core of the forging remaining and every bit of the rod's surface polished. Indeed Rolls-Royce claimed that every component of the car, when it was not machined, was filed and polished all over to find flaws or cracks in the metal, and every highly stressed piece was examined with a magnifying glass to discover surface cracks. Flaw detection was in its infancy in those days of course, and even twenty years later Rolls-Royce were somewhat behind the times in their detection methods. On the other hand they were ahead of their time in the measures they took to prevent flaws rather than tracing them:

Ghosts could still be very high even in 1914, like this landaulette

The Ghost reached a different kind of zenith in the form of the Alpine Eagle, this 1914 tourer–bodied version representing the popular British ideal of a fast Rolls–Royce

all clearance and lightening holes bored in brackets and tubes were carefully machined to a smooth finish, for instance, so as to avoid the possibility of a rough finish starting a fracture, and the common practice of stamping the chassis number on one of the main frame members was shunned because the stamping might weaken the member.

Rolls-Royce really were most distrustful of other people's methods. Because of this they made everything possible themselves, even every nut, taking care to ensure that the tapped hole was square with the abutment face, and testing and if necessary re-tempering all spring washers that in any case were only used for locking external nuts, internal ones always being castellated and locked with cotter pins or by similar positive methods. All rotating parts were balanced, not just the wheels, crankshaft and flywheel but also all gear wheels and even the bevel gears in the final drive Copper pipes were brazed, not merely soldered. Rods and tubes in tension were always straight. Everything ferrous was steel except the cast iron cylinders, piston rings and the brake linings for the handbrake; and the steel parts were always rolled steel or forgings, except for four particular pieces which could only be cast. In every little detail, manifest or concealed, perfection was sought. The

Claude Johnson

quality would still be appreciated, as Royce was so fond of remarking, long after the price had been forgotten.

The difficulty lay in persuading a potential customer, who could only see the price, of the quality which perhaps he could not see. Of course everything possible was done to ensure a perfect finish, such as might convince him that he was contemplating something especially good. In particular the nickel plating was of a quality unmatched by that of any other motor car manufacturer, simply because no other employed the Rolls-Royce technique of close plating. The commonly accepted system was electro-plating, but Royce despised the microscopically thin layer of nickel left by electro deposition, and instead employed craftsmen in cutting to shape pure nickel sheet about 0.006-inch thick and then soldering it on to the part to be plated. This Sheffield plating keeps its colour permanently, does not scrape off, and has an almost indefinite life.

But could the prospective purchaser tell the difference between close plating and electroplating when the work was new? Would he appreciate the advantages in stress distribution secured by assembling the axle casing with a large number of small studs rather than with a few big ones? Would he appreciate the care with which the brake linings were hand bedded to their respective drums? He might prefer to have one of the rival cars with four-wheel brakes, which Rolls-Royce were still not providing despite their growing popularity on the better of the continental makes and indeed some pre-war British ones.

In fact Royce was well aware of the need for four-wheel brakes, and had been working on them for a very long time before it was announced in November 1923 that the Ghost would now have four-wheel brakes, augmented by a servo motor that had been adapted from the Hispano Suiza example. The system

Even in 1914, foreign bodies were gracing Ghosts with commendable success. It would be very difficult to improve this Mühlbachen double brougham on an Alpine Eagle chassis

was overdue, but, as was usually the case with Rolls-Royce, it was late in coming because a lot of time was necessary to ensure that it was as good as it could be.

This change in the braking system was the last significant alteration to the Ghost, being preceded in 1919 by the adoption of electric lighting and starting sets, as previously noted. The story is told of a man who presented himself on the Rolls-Royce stand at the Motor Show in that year, explaining that he had no previous experience of motor cars and no particular taste for them, pre-ferring horses, but that he recognised nevertheless that the motor car was now a practical necessity rather than a luxury. 'However', he continued, 'I have no mechanical knowledge what-ever and cannot yet consider buying myself a car unless I can be assured of its infallible reliability. The Rolls-Royce, I am given to understand, is perfectly reliable ; and I would consider buying one if I could be assured of this.' The salesman, warming to what pro-mised to be an easy task, took the potential customer for a conducted tour of the exhibition chassis and in due course they came around to the front where the customer pointed down be-tween the chassis dumb irons and asked 'What's that handle thing down there ?'

Carelessly the salesman replied 'That, sir, is the starting handle.'

'I see' said the customer, 'you told me earlier that this car had a self-starter ; but it now appears that the con-fidence of Rolls-Royce in their own mechanism is so tenuous that a starting handle has to be made available for the eventuality of the self-starter failing. I am bitterly disappointed, for I see that the time for me to begin motoring has not yet come.'

The salesman thought rapidly. 'Sir,' said he, 'have you ever noticed, when in your bath, you have a couple of little nipple things on your chest ?'

'I have,' snapped the customer 'what of it ?'

'Sir, they were put there to cater for the possibility of your one day having a baby. Sir, the chances of your requiring to use the starting handle on the Rolls-Royce are no greater.'

London–Edinburgh chassis adapted by E W Hives (later Lord Hives) and raced at Brooklands in 1911

THE WAR TO END ALL WARS

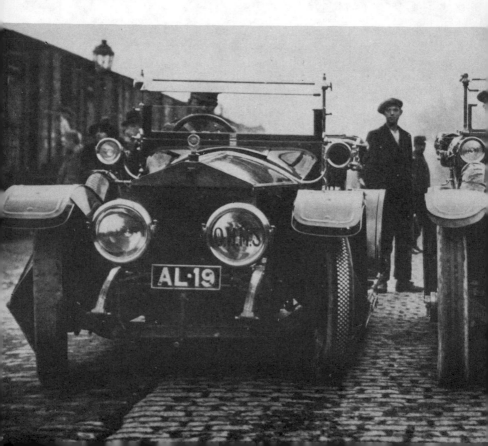

When the Great War erupted, mobilisation and mechanisation were not synonymous. The contestant armies were very poorly equipped with mechanical transport, and many of those in charge of them had very little appreciation of its value. As far as the British army was concerned, many of its leaders began their studies of war with the ability to scan and construe that notorious line *quadrupedantem putrem sonitu quatit ungula campi;* and many thousands of hapless quadrupeds laboured miserably and perished horribly. Heavy transport had been organised to a limited extent, though it was useless on soft ground; armoured fighting vehicles were simply non-existent. It did not take long, however, before the bigger and stronger private cars that had been in production in the immediate prewar years were adapted to the purposes of war. Things as varied as the Model T Ford, the Vauxhall 23/60, and the Crossley and others were pressed into service as staff cars and as tenders, especially for the Royal Flying Corps. As was to be expected, Rolls-Royce chassis were reserved for the most glamorous or the most arduous duties, in recognition of their qualities. Because of its performance and reliability, it was a Rolls-Royce that dashed about all over France at very high speeds carrying the King's Messenger. Because of the size, the ride quality and perhaps the quietness of the Silver Ghost, many examples were converted to ambulances; and because of the capacity of the Rolls-Royce for taking punishment, it served as the basis of the most successful armoured car to see service during the war.

On His Majesty's Service, three of the four King's Messengers with their cars at Boulogne: left to right, Charles Hardy (chassis number 4), Maynard Bryant (2047), and Barry (737, called Silver Rogue)

It was not the only one to be good – there were some Lanchesters that did well in Russia, for example – but it was the only one to be blessed with a glamorous reputation, though this only spread some years later upon the publication of Lawrence's *Seven Pillars of Wisdom*. In this book the armoured Silver Ghost is given unstinting praise, by a man who knew good machinery and could handle it. Despite the weight of armour and equipment being twice what the chassis was designed to carry, despite the need for the radiator to be masked with armoured shutters when it went into action, despite the tremendous heat of Palestine, Arabia and Libya where these vehicles did such notable work, the Silver Ghost chassis proved incredibly reliable. Engine wear was slight, engine failure unheard of, and most of the running gear was equally dependable apart from an occasional problem with hub bearings. Tyres, for which Rolls-Royce could not take any responsibility, inevitably gave trouble, either because of the enormous loads they had to carry at speeds up to 60mph (which might be sustained over long

Lawrence of Arabia in Damascus

Above: Ghost armoured cars on patrol in Palestine
Below: Some of the RR armoured cars remained in service for decades after the First World War

distances in the desert), or on account of the rough surfaces over which they ran, or from time to time on account of punctures from bullets.

The original Rolls-Royce armoured cars, which were first commissioned by the Royal Naval Air Service, ran on solid tyres because of the weight problem; later, twin rear wheels were found to be a sufficient insurance against overload problems and the pneumatic came back into its own, being naturally far better on sand and other soft terrain. But it was not only in the Middle East that these fighting Ghosts fought so well: they gave equally faithful service in Russia, in France, in German West Africa and at Gallipoli. After the war ended they went on to see further service in India and Afghanistan and even further East. Westerly they had not so far to travel: they served in Ireland.

The impeccable performance of these cars may be seen either as a tribute to faultless workmanship or an example of the occasional rewards of over-insurance. The Silver Ghost chassis was successful as the basis of an armoured car because it was developed to stand an enormous degree of overload and an incredible amount of abuse. Whether it is desirable that a private motor car should be so constructed as never to overheat when carrying two tons of armour plating at high speeds in the North African desert with its radiator shuttered is questionable, since the uses for which it was presumably intended involved lighter loads, lower engine temperatures and a deliberate flaunting of that unmistakable radiator. As has been said before, the Rolls-Royce had to be designed to accommodate the shortcomings of any conceivable driver, and indeed we may have the low standard of skill of the pre-war motorist to thank for our successes in several fields of battle.

Nevertheless the principal contribution of Rolls-Royce to the war effort was not in the provision of armoured car chassis but in the development of a new range of aero engines. Once again it was reliability which distinguished them: the average aero engine in 1915 had an overhaul life of not more than twenty hours, and in the case of the majority of rotary engines this was often nearer five hours. The greatest contribution made by Rolls-Royce to the art of aero engine design and manufacture was to raise these figures to something like 150 hours initially and later to even longer periods of service.

A certain amount of resistance had to be overcome before Rolls-Royce would take any part in aviation whatsoever. Henry Royce was averse to the whole idea, due (it was believed) to his association of flying with the death of Rolls. Even before the war broke out in 1914 Claude Johnson had tried to interest Royce in aero engines, but without any success. When the war came along the situation was obviously different, and pressure was brought to bear in the various other ways that Government had.

To begin with, it was arranged that Rolls-Royce should produce aero engines of the Renault type and the successors to this design that were under development at the Royal Aircraft Factory. The Renault and most of the RAF engines were air-cooled V8s of poor performance and frightful thirst having to be virtually fuel-cooled with very rich mixtures in order to avoid the hazards of gross overheating to which they could easily succumb. Royce at any rate was horrified by them, and decided that if he were to make aero engines he would make good ones. So when the Admiralty came to him with pressing requirements he responded with more enthusiasm than he had hitherto shown, and undertook to design an engine that would have much greater endurance than contemporary engines displayed while developing something like 75 or perhaps 100hp.

This engine was to become known as the Hawk, and the way that Royce set about designing it showed that he was perfectly well aware of the limitations in his motor car engines, limitations which were after all deliberately built into the design. He knew that the Silver Ghost engine was mechanically sound and he knew that its volumetric efficiency was low. The means of obtaining high volumetric efficiency were already known, for the racing cars of the immediate pre-war period, mostly based on the pioneering work of Henry and Peugeot, were getting good results from overhead camshaft layouts with inclined opposed valves in crossflow cylinder heads. The Admiralty had acquired one of the engines that had powered the Mercédès Grand Prix car which had dominated the Grand Prix of the Automobile Club of France held in 1914 on 5th July at Lyon (it was rumoured that W O Bentley, given a Naval commission during the war, had something to do with their acquisition of this engine; but at any rate it has been recorded that one Briggs, a naval officer concerned with engines, took it from the Mercédès showroom on 4th August and thence to Derby) and they handed it over to Royce. What he did then was simply to copy the cylinder head (a welded fabrication, as were the cylinders and water jackets of the German design) and valve mechanism of the Mercédès engine, superimposing this on the bottom half of the six-cylinder Rolls-Royce Silver Ghost. The much better breathing of the new cylinder head was sufficient to raise the power of the engine from 53 to 75hp at 1,350 rev/min.

All this was encompassed by the early spring of 1915. The design was then shelved because there were more urgent military requirements to be satisfied. Rolls-Royce were being asked for a 200hp engine, and it was wanted in a hurry. So Royce and his chief assistant, Elliot (who had come from Napier) set about the design, reasoning that the way to get the desired results was to double the 6-cylinder Hawk engine so as to produce a V12, at the same time lengthening the stroke from $4\frac{3}{4}$ to $6\frac{1}{2}$-inches. This would increase the swept volume to rather more than 20-litres,

Ghost production for the domestic market was considerably cut back as the war continued

which should suffice to give the required power with Rolls-Royce reliability. Work started on the drawings in April 1915; in October the prototype engine gave 225hp on the dynamometer.

This engine was christened the Eagle, and it was really a prodigy of concentrated effort and high-speed development. Most of the work was done by Royce and Elliot unassisted, though as usual Royce was not too proud to farm out mathematical and scientific problems to consultants. Six months was extraordinarily brief a gestation for any engine, let alone a high-powered aero engine, and for it to deliver 225hp when only 200 had been specified seemed to set the seal on a tremendous achievement. Yet in a sense the Eagle gave too little and too late, for by the time it was proving itself on the test bench the government was asking for more power. By the following March, therefore, the power of the Eagle was raised to 266hp; by July it had risen to 284hp; and by the end of the year it stood at no less than 322. At that stage the engine was put into production and in fact it remained in service from 1917 until well into the

Sometime in the mid-twenties Royce
posed for the camera in this Ghost

1930s. Its power output continued to grow: by September 1917 it stood at 350hp, and ten more were added within the next five months. Indeed the Eagle seemed destined for great things as the war drew on into 1918, for a new generation of heavy long-range bombers had been planned and this engine was the obvious one to power them, having both the ability and the reliability. The Handley Page 0/400, the Vickers Vimy and early versions of the ill-fated Handley Page V/1500 were all earmarked for the Eagle, as were several other flying boats and bombers.

As it happened, the Eagle's greatest exploit took place after the war was over: the Vickers Vimy which successfully completed the first nonstop flight across the Atlantic in the hands of Alcock and Whitten Brown in 1919 provided the most dramatic demonstration of the engine's reliability, though as we shall later see the Eagle was not without its long-range shortcomings.

It was in any case an unadventurous design. The power increases that it enjoyed during its long career were achieved by straightforward development and little or nothing revolutionary. Basically the Eagle was a water-cooled 60° V12, with each cylinder formed as a separate unit with its own water jacket. Each cylinder barrel was machined from a steel forging, as were the exhaust and inlet ports which were then welded onto the head. This was standard Mercédès practice, as was the location of the single camshaft in a casing along the top of each bank of cylinders, where it could through rockers conveniently operate the inclined opposed valves. Four 6-cylinder magnetos fed the sparking plugs (two to each cylinder) and German practice was further emulated in the articulation of the connecting rods, this being the most convenient way of converting an in-line six into a V12. Where the Rolls-Royce was greatly superior to the Daimler and indeed to most others was in its reduction gear, an apparatus which too many aero engine manufac-

turers were still convinced was unnecessary. The Germans recognised the value of reduction gear in permitting more efficient exploitation of airscrews, but they used crude spur gears; Royce incorporated an epicyclic reduction gear which was much kinder to the crankcase structure and made its own contribution to long overhaul life.

Indeed the Eagle was tremendously reliable and yet not too heavy. Its weight was less than 860 lb, and when this is related to its power output in late 1917 or early 1918 it can be seen that the specific weight of the Eagle was, despite the natural tendency of a liquid-cooled in-line engine to be heavy, comparable with the best that was being achieved by air-cooled engines of inferior performance and reliability. The specific fuel consumption was not particularly good, about $\frac{2}{3}$ of a pound of petrol per horsepower hour. The oil consumption was, however, decidedly modest by the standards of the time, amounting to a mere gallon per hour. Most other engines of the time could scarcely have been provisioned with sufficient oil had they been able to run for as long as the Eagle, which would keep on keeping on for hours at its rated power, though another 200 rev/min would bring about its failure if sustained for even five minutes.

Even before the Eagle had gone into production, Rolls-Royce were being pestered for yet another engine. This time the government were asking for 190hp, and Royce decided that the way to achieve this was to design a scaled-down version of the Eagle. He called this the Falcon, and in designing it he must have taken into account the evident tendency of governmental departments to underestimate their requirements. In this he was justified, for once again the power output had to be increased: in April 1916 the figure was 205hp, and month later it was 228hp. Nine months after that it had gone up to 217hp and by April 1917 it was 262hp, still at the original 1,800 rev/min.

Above: The submarine-hunting dirigible airship played a far more vital role in the First World War than is generally recognised, and the RR Hawk engine's reliability was the cornerstone of its success. SS 'Z59' is being flown from the deck of HMS 'Furious'

Below: Designed after the Hawk, the Eagle went into production earlier. Various stages in its construction are shown in this 1916 picture of the Nightingale Road works at Derby

Towards the end of the First World War a new generation of long-range heavy bombers was developed, all relying on the RR V12 series of aero-engines. Eagles powered this one, the Vickers Vimy

Before the end of the war the power of the Falcon had risen to 285hp at 2,000 rev/min, the engine weighing between 650 and 700 lb according to type.

Whereas the Eagle was intended for heavy bombers, the Falcon was for a new breed of heavy fighters: the Mark III version of it was put into production for the superb new Bristol fighter, to remain standard and in service until the 1930s, and only after the Falcon was put into production could the little old six-cylinder Hawk be revived. This had

originally been intended to power training aircraft, but now the Admiralty had a first-class panic on about the German submarines which were crippling the British mercantile fleet and making what threatened to be a successful bid to finish the war completely. The idea of hunting these U-boats from the air had suddenly been recognised as a good one, and so there was an urgent need for an engine that could churn on for hours on end propelling a submarine-hunting airship.

These airships, the SS Zero class, were operated by the Royal Naval Air Service. They were disarmingly simple, consisting of a Blimp-like gas envelope from which was suspended a long nacelle that looked like a contemporary aircraft fuselage shorn of its wings

imple it may have been and slow it lmost certainly was, but this type of irship was amazingly effective. The NAS flew them for a total of 36,000 ours, on one occasion in August 1918 ogging a continuous sortie of fifty hours fty-five minutes. Patrols lasting twenty-iree to thirty hours were quite com-non, and it was no coincidence that the ctivity of these anti-submarine air-nips coincided with a reduction in inkings of Allied ships by German ubmarines. It is difficult to think of any ther manufacturer capable of produc-ng an engine so suitable as the Rolls-oyce for these duties, where long-uration reliability was of paramount nportance.

To be fair, it is difficult to think of nything other than this reliability to distinguish the Hawk or indeed any of the aero engines that Rolls-Royce pro-produced during the Great War. They were old-fashioned in design, for the separate cylinder construction had been made obsolete in 1915 when Hispano Suiza introduced a water-cooled V8 of monobloc construction, the cylinder banks being extremely stiff aluminium castings crowned by heads within which the overhead camshaft gear was completely enclosed and lubricated with oil that would then be returned to the crankcase. Indeed the British had an aero engine with enclosed lubricated valve gear before the war began (an experimental proto-type by Green) but while the Italians and the Germans continued with their more old-fashioned design one could

After the First World War had
ended, RR put a Hawk aero-engine
in a Ghost chassis, but found it
too noisy for their market. Lt Col
G H Henderson went one better,
putting a 14-litre RR Falcon aero-
engine and RR radiator to a Napier
chassis which was old even then,
to make this curious roadburner

not expect any revolutionary modernity from Rolls-Royce. In the case of the Germans at least there was an essential difference, in that they were doing serious work with supercharging enabling their engines to operate effectively at greater altitudes than could any Allied one. The Royal Aircraft Factory was hard at work on this new principle, as were the French; Royce as ever stuck to making what he knew and making it as well as he knew how. This was the way to achieve reliability.

Nevertheless it was reliability of a different order from that which distinguished the Silver Ghost. The aero engines could not tolerate abuse and overload in the same way that the car engine could: the abrupt curtailment of the Eagle's operational life it it were run at 200 rev/min above the rated figure showed this quite clearly. Indeed the Eagle and the Falcon could turn quite nasty if not operated strictly in accordance with instructions. The Eagle in particular suffered from severe torsional vibration of the crankshaft at certain engine speeds. It was the old problem again, and the old solution was applied: a friction damper, consisting of a multi-plate clutch, was built into the reduction gear housing. This damper successfully dealt with the problems of torsional flutter, but not before the war had finished. This could make things very awkward, especially in long-range flights: for example the most economical cruising speed of the Mark 8 Eagle engines, such as powered the Vickers Vimy of Alcock and Brown, was 1,750 rev/min; but this speed coincided with a serious torsional harmonic in engines not equipped with the damper, so that in them it could not be

used continuously. Yet, as we have seen, the peak power output of the Eagle was yielded at 1,800 rev/min, at which speed the engine could operate reliably for a reasonably long period. Clearly the reliability of the engine was balanced most precariously on a knife edge.

So are the fortunes of war. All the other protagonists with their in-line 6-cylinder engines and V12s were suffering similar difficulties, and none of them could do better than Rolls-Royce in terms of long overhaul life even though the Daimler and Benz engines of the Germans could fly higher, while Fiat's biggest engine was more powerful. The French were generally averse to sixes and twelves, though some of their eights were pretty treacherous (notably the Bugatti, which was built as a double eight) while the Americans had no idea of how to go about making aero engines at all and made a hideous mess of everything, designing the Liberty as a V8 and producing it as a half-baked V12 too late to be of any use – or, which is another way of thinking about it, too late to do any great harm. Meanwhile, as the final months dragged on in 1918, the Hawks were pinning down Germany's submarines, the Eagle was installed in the huge Handley Page bomber that was to bring destruction to Berlin (but was erroneously flown to and landed in German territory before it ever became operational), and the Falcon was being regularly installed in Bristol fighters. It is just a little like poetic justice that when eventually Bristol came to make their own aero engines they were the first to master the problems of crankshaft vibration. Maybe what was to happen half a century later, when Bristol fell into the clutches of Rolls-Royce, was poetic injustice ...

MAMMON'S MOTORS

During the Great War, plans were made for the production of Rolls-Royce aero engines in America. A number of technicians had been sent there from Derby in order to supervise the setting up of manufactories and the training of American workmen in Rolls-Royce methods. Everything was going well; but fortunately the war went better, and the Armistice was celebrated before any American-built Rolls-Royce engine went into active service. It seemed a pity to Rolls-Royce that the organisation thus established, not to mention the goodwill, should be wasted and forgotten; and it seemed an even better idea that the vicious tariffs imposed by the Americans on the import of cars from overseas might be circumvented by the manufacture of Rolls-Royce Silver Ghosts actually in America. Johnson pursued this idea enthusiastically, and in November 1919 the ranks of American car manufacturers were swelled by Rolls-Royce of America Incorporated, capitalized to the tune of £800,000 and

substantially under the control of th British company. A factory was a quired at Springfield, Massachusetts, further body of men was sent out fro Derby (bringing the total to fift three) and the Silver Ghost was p into production.

If it seemed a good idea at the tim Johnson had not allowed for the effect snob appeal, a factor which was alwa important in the sale of cars in gener and Rolls-Royce cars in particula American customers showed an unfo tunate and unexpected tendency treat the Springfield product as imitation Rolls-Royce, a cheap su stitute for the real British-built thing and perversely they wanted to buy th Derby Ghosts, not the Springfield one A great campaign was therefo launched in order to convince th appropriate sector of the America public that the Silver Ghosts built Massachusetts were mechanically ide tical to those from Derbyshire, we

Sir Henry Royce

Above: Horizontal radiator slats mark the early 20hp 'baby' RR
Below: The later 20/25 hp model looked more like its bigger brethren

produced subject to the same discipline, and were bodied in styles that were complementary in elegance and excellence even though the eleven assorted standard versions were made in the United States by Brewster (a first-class coachbuilder whom Rolls-Royce were soon to acquire). In fact practically everything was made in America except the crankshafts, the Ferodo brake linings, and one or two odds and ends. The metals employed were produced to Rolls-Royce specification and, as at Derby, every casting and forging had an integral test piece upon which sundry metallurgical checks were made so as to ensure the integrity of the finished component.

The same painstaking routine of fitting and testing was followed in Springfield as in Derby, including the mechanised bump testing of the chassis and suspension and the final testing of the whole car on a special chassis dynamometer so that the installed power could be checked. To begin with, the engine and transmission were run light for about four hours, followed by a two-hour session including a check on full-throttle maximum power. This was only the beginning of a very complicated test sequence through which every car was put after leaving the assembly shop, before it could be passed for delivery to the owner.

What followed would have been enough to put the producer of any lesser car out of business. First there was a road test of 100 to 150 miles for silence and general functioning, after which the chassis was completely dismantled and everything inspected. After it was all put together again there was a second dynamometer test for power, carburation and general performance, followed by a short road run as a double check. Then the engine had its turn to be dismantled, cleaned, given a valve grind and final painting and checking. Final inspection for performance followed in a road test of one hundred miles, or more if necessary, after which the chassis was again inspected before being delivered

to the coachbuilding department for the mounting of the body. When the body had been given an initial painting, the completed car was given a further road test of one-hundred miles or more in order that the body could 'shake down' (an expression that has horrifying and altogether inappropriate connotations) after which there was a final inspection of the whole car before finish-painting and trim.

In this way the Springfield factory produced 1,703 Silver Ghosts, a figure that compares quite respectably with the Derby output quoted in an earlier chapter.

Things were becoming difficult, however, on both sides of the Atlantic. Rolls-Royce may have enjoyed raping the luxury car market in the boom years immediately following the war, but by 1921 post-rape depression was beginning to set in and sales were falling so much that the company was tempted to think that the odd twenty or thirty thousand pounds it might get from the government for an aero engine development contract might be well worth having. Yet even supposing they got it – and before long they did – it would not keep the expanded organisation going: something had to be done to restore the lost motor-car business. If its customers were rebuffing approaches made with that sacred monster the Silver Ghost. then more customers would have to be found for a cheaper and smaller Rolls-Royce – though not, emphatically not, one that was in any way inferior in behaviour or quality.

Royce decided that a smaller engine giving about 50hp would be needed, and design work was put in hand in 1919. The engine was again to be an in-line six, again with a stroke of $4\frac{1}{2}$ inches like that of the original 40/50 (though after 1909 the stroke of the Ghost engine had been increased by a quarter of an inch to bring its capacity to $7,428cm^3$). This prototype engine was to have a bore of three inches, so that the RAC horsepower rating was 20.6, about half that of the Silver Ghost. Like

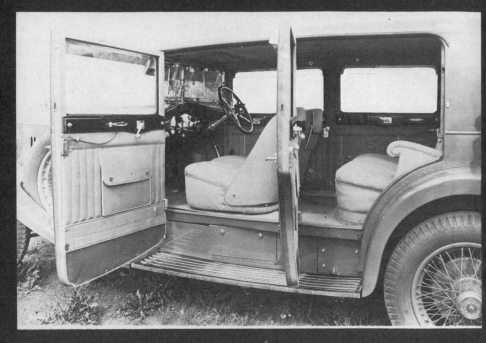

Above: Weymann bodies, the most cleverly constructed of the time, looked handsome inside and out, like this 1929 specimen on a Phantom 1 Below: American coachbuilders did some fine work on Springfield-built Phantom 1 chassis. Murphy's cabriolet was inspired by Gangloff of France

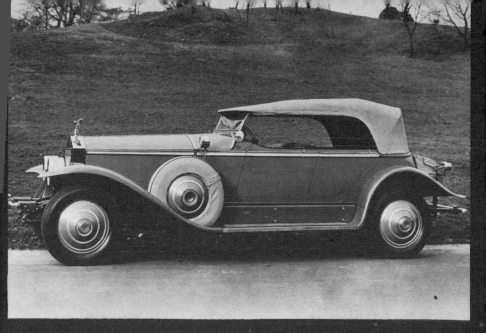

Above: Purely American in style is this phaeton body on a Springfield Phantom 1, Brewster's Derby Speedster
Below: Only the slightly higher radiator betrays this Phantom 1 as a Springfield car; it is bodied to a Darrin design

its predecessor it had a seven-bearing crankshaft, of meagre proportions and giving no evidence that its designers were aware of the problems of dynamic balance or torsional rigidity such as are peculiar to a six-crank shaft. On the other hand the valve gear was quite adventurous, incorporating two overhead camshafts; and if only the sales department had not been so importunate in demanding that the car be ready for production in the autumn of 1922, it is possible that this ohc layout might have been developed to the necessary degree of quietness and general practicality, in which case the course of Rolls-Royce engineering might well have taken a very different heading. What happened instead was that the camshaft was put back into the crankcase and left to communicate its dictates to the overhead valves through pushrods and rockers. The traditional Rolls-Royce all-speed governor which had been present on the prototype engine (known as the Goshawk) was deleted, and the whole engine was built in unit with the gearbox, the entire sub-assembly being mounted in a U-shaped sub-frame attached to the chassis at three points.

The gearbox mustered three forward speeds, and the gear lever together with the handbrake lever sprouted from the centre of the floor. This was immediately condemned as rank heresy if not (which was even worse) vulgarity when the car appeared in 1922; and in 1925 Rolls-Royce bowed before the storm and substituted a four-speed gearbox with the levers to the right of the driver.

The height of elegance was achieved in bodies created for the Phantom 2. This Weymann coupé is wonderfully restrained and yet wholly purposeful

1930 Springfield Phantom 1
supporting a very restrained but
sporty 'York' body by Brewster

Another feature of the design, less obvious to the average customer though more objectionable to the discerning engineer, was the adoption of Hotchkiss drive, presumably because it was so much cheaper and simpler than the torque-tube axle location of the Silver Ghost. The traction of the car did not really suffer, for it was neither so light nor so powerful that this might be any kind of problem; but the handling certainly did suffer – a matter which caused buyers not the slightest concern, for they were no more likely to drive the new 'small' or 20hp Rolls in a sporting manner around corners or along winding roads than they were to make free use of the four-speed gearbox they had so self-righteously and hypocritically demanded. All they wanted was to sit in a plushy body behind a genuine Rolls-Royce radiator.

Some of the bodies reached a level of sumptuousness and correspondingly of weight that was quite out of keeping with the size of the chassis, the power of the engine or the intentions of its manufacturer. Some allowance for these impositions was made by the choice of final drive ratios, but the putting-on-weight syndrome affected the 20 just as it did every other car that Rolls-Royce made. This may have proved something about the sort of people who bought Rolls-Royce cars, and it was undoubtedly one of the reasons why there would never again be such a long unbroken run for a single model as the Silver Ghost had enjoyed. Johnson had been responsible for the one-car policy, and his judgement on that occasion was perfect: it was by concentrating on the Silver Ghost and giving it a reputation that did not have to be compromised by other considerations for some years that the company had been built into such a strong one. The introduction of the 'baby Rolls' in 1922 indicated that things were now going to be very different.

The fact that the Silver Ghost had suffered from the same problems of increasing weight and diminishing performance, at a time when it was already getting old and therefore unable to keep pace with the splendid new high-powered luxury cars coming on the market from such manufacturers as Hispano-Suiza, forced Rolls-Royce into giving it a new engine. It was not very different in capacity from that of the Ghost, though the cylinder bores were much smaller and the stroke considerably greater; but it had overhead valve gear like that of the 20 and the consequent increase in power restored the performance of the car to more tolerable levels. What with the new engine and other recent detail changes, it was time for the name of the Silver Ghost to be dropped: its successor was named the New Phantom. It was faster, taller, uglier and more ponderous than its predecessor and enjoyed a short life, going out of production in 1929. On the other hand it was quite a success in America, where the Springfield factory had its best year in 1928, selling nearly 400 of this model.

Unfortunately for Rolls-Royce of America, it was doomed never to proceed to the new Phantom's successor, the Phantom 2. When that car made its appearance in 1929 it was deemed too complex an undertaking to be put into production at Springfield, where the changeover to the new Phantom from the Silver Ghost was relatively simple since the only major alteration was the engine. So the American sales went into a steady decline, for if American customers were so snobbish that they had to be talked out of buying an English-built Rolls-Royce, they were certainly not going to be fobbed off with an obsolete model. In any case the American slump had already taken its toll of the market, and sales in 1929 were only half of what they were in the previous year. In 1930 they were halved again and the number of imported Rolls-Royce also suffered a sharp drop. The following year, production stopped in Massachusetts; and in 1934 Rolls-Royce of America Incorporated died of bankruptcy, eight years after the death of Claude Johnson who had done so much to give it life.

Going from the coupé to this sedanca de ville, we still see the fine basic proportions of the Phantom 2 guiding the coachbuilder to success . . .

. . and the effect persists even in the full-length limousine

The Phantom 2 could carry gracefully the curves that were to become a feature of the later 1930s

Even on the Phantom 2, things could still go wrong, as this 1932 Cholmondeley sportsman's saloon proves

The changes made to the large and small Rolls-Royce in 1929 were interesting but hardly stimulating. The engine of the 20 was bored out by a quarter of an inch; and a new crankshaft with larger journals and crankpins and yet another design of torsional vibration damper (this particular design problem had exercised the company's engineers vigorously throughout the previous decade) allowed that rev/min could rise to 4,000. Compression ratio was raised, and the gearbox was equipped with synchromesh on third and fourth gears so that timid drivers could now risk starting off in second gear rather than third and if feeling adventurous might even try a downward change from top gear while the car was still moving. Later a constant-mesh or 'silent' second gear was added to the specification and a few even more

minor changes were made; but apart from its engine the small ·Rolls remained essentially similar to the original 20, confirming that the design of that model had been shrewdly judged to suit the envisaged market.

Some disquiet was felt and occasionally expressed at the more considerable changes effected in the Phantom, for the Phantom 2 chassis had more in common with the small Rolls than with previous big ones. The torque-tube location of the rear axle went, leaving that heavy but excitable component to the mercies of simple half-elliptic springs and Hotchkiss drive. This seemed to indicate a decline in standards, though in fact the P2 handled better than the P1. In sundry ways the new car was more practical: for example it adopted the one-shot centralised lubrication that had been a Springfield innovation, substituting the occasional booting of a pedal by the driver for the weekly lubrication of about a hundred points on the pre-war Silver Ghost.

Another feature of the P2 that it boasted in common with the 20/25 was synchromesh on third and top gears, and many drivers were immensely relieved that the system of notches locking the gear lever into engagement had been abandoned, making a smooth and reasonably quick gearchange much easier.

Remembering other things from the Silver Ghost days, Rolls-Royce put into production an additional version of the P2 known as the Continental, and distinguished by its short wheelbase of only 12 feet instead of 12½. This chassis carried some of the most handsome bodies ever to grace any motor car, and when it was suitably bodied the P2 Continental was readily capable of a genuine 90mph or more. In achieving this it was encouraged by a developed version of the original Phantom engine, now with a one-piece detachable aluminium-alloy cylinder head with crossflow porting and greatly improved inlet and exhaust manifolds. Many felt that this engine lacked the smoothness of earlier Royce big sixes, and the factory mechanics used to call it 'Gutty rough'. At least it was more powerful than the earlier engine, and the illusion of lost refinement may merely have been the consequence of this fact. Indeed the engine of the P2 was quite happy to rev, and the car responded very well to the free use of the gearbox though it was still perfectly capable of dawdling along at 5mph in top gear.

There were some few customers who were quite content with the coarse appeal of the new car in return for the greatly improved performance. However, if they were attracted by this sort of thing they were just as likely to be attracted by the latest Bentleys. These now had six cylinders, were flexible, quieter than they used to be, and were a good deal faster than the Rolls-Royce. The 6½-litre might not be as glamorous as the Speed 6 which had won the 24-hour race at Le Mans in 1929 and which did so again in 1930, vanquishing an opponent no less renowned than Mercédès; but it was also a good deal less glamorous than the thundering great sports car, and there were plenty of men prepared to put up with Bentley performance that was not all that much better than that of a Rolls-Royce in order to bask in the reflected glory that came the way of the great green cars in France. Then in 1930 when Bentley's crowning glory, the 8-litre car, came along – practically as quiet as a Rolls-Royce in its own way, looking as impressive, and with a much higher performance – Rolls-Royce had cause for concern.

They also had reason to comfort themselves, for the Bentley company was in dire financial straits, the depression of the British market hitting all other manufacturers of luxury cars before it hit Rolls-Royce who were soundly established and could always look to the establishment for custom when their rivals had to go out and create customers. By 1931 Bentley's finances were in an even more precarious condition and eventually the inevitable happened: the firm went broke.

This was a matter of considerable interest not only to Rolls-Royce but also to Napier. Napier had given up the production of motor cars in 1925, when they abandoned their own 40/50hp car, one which like the Rolls-Royce had a smooth-running 6-cylinder engine, but which had a technical specification that included such niceties as an aluminium alloy cylinder block, an overhead camshaft, and some pretence to aero engine standards of manufacture and design. Unfortunately the Napier did not go as well as it should have done, with the natural if literally paradoxical consequence that it went, leaving Napier without a car in production or even on the drawing board. They were quite keen to get back into the motor car business, for the aviation world was beginning to treat them somewhat impatiently: their managing director H T Vane was too bemused by the past success of their Lion aero engine to recognise that it had come

73

Drum headlights and rolled bumpers are two outstanding features of the Springfield built models

Most bizarre of all, this Brewster 'Windswept' sport saloon was built on a Phantom 2 chassis for the 1933 World's Fair at Chicago . . .

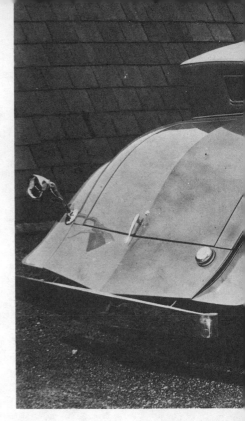

very near to the limits of its development. It seemed so well established that he judged it the ultimate aircraft engine that would remain on the market for ever and ever.

If Vane and his fellow directors thought thus, the British Government, who signed most of the cheques for aero engine development in the UK at that time (as at most others), thought differently: they did not view the Lion with special favour and had little confidence in its future potential. They had asked Napier to develop a supercharged version but Napier had done little or nothing about it, though toying briefly with a supercharged V12 whose design was in many respects retrogressive. As recounted in another chapter, the Air Ministry felt constrained and even encouraged to take their business more to Rolls-Royce and less to Napier in the future: so the great and long-established rivalry between these two companies became more embittered and Napier were understandably enthusiastic about the idea of getting back into the car business on the basis of the work that Bentley had already done.

When Bentley Motors Limited went into liquidation, Napier entered negotiations with them and with W O Bentley himself, and plans were drawn up for Napier to buy the assets of the Bentley company and put into production a developed version of the magnificent 8-litre, to be known as the Bentley Napier. This was courageous, in view of the economic situation prevailing at the time, but it has always seemed an inspired idea that was almost certain to succeed. Alas, one of those many slips that occur 'twixt cup and lip brought all these carefully laid plans to nothing. When all the negotiations had been completed there remained the formal requirement of an appearance by both parties before

the Receiver's Court, where the proposed arrangements might be given judicial approval. Counsel for Napiers explained the agreed proposals – and then another lawyer, never previously seen and scarcely noted on this occasion since he was not a man of any reputation, rose and put it to the court that he acted for the British Central Equitable Trust and that his instructions were to offer a larger sum for the assets of Bentley Motors Limited than Napier had proposed.

This was a bombshell. Nobody present had ever heard of the British Central Equitable Trust, nor could they imagine whom the name might conceal. The whole manoeuvre was a surprise, perfectly timed and apparently exe-

. . . and featured such uncharacteristic things as scuttle-less bonnet, apparently unparkable screen-wipers, and folding front seats which really looked inviting

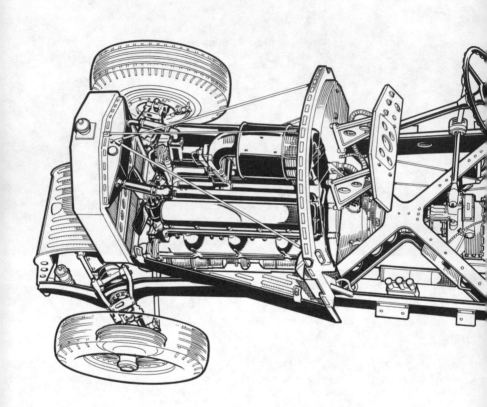

Cutaway of the 1935 Phantom 3

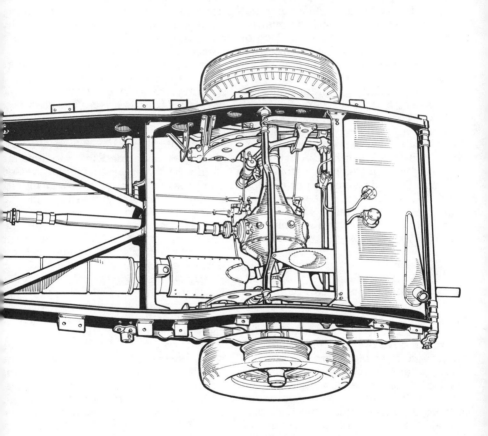

cuted with no little skill, for Napier's counsel was evidently taken aback: he asked for time to consult his clients, feeling sure that they would increase their bid, for the differences in the prices offered was quite marginal and the court ought surely to take into account the fact that all other aspects of the negotiations had been satisfactorily concluded. The judge took a different view, indicating with some acidity that it was not his office to preside over an auction – and then flying in the face of his own declaration by saying that since the first duty of the Receiver's Court was to look to the interest of the creditors, the British Central Equitable Trust's offer had to be accepted.

A week later W O Bentley learned that the mysterious intervention had been made on behalf of Rolls-Royce; and a little later still he discovered at first hand what it was like to work for a big, wealthy and ruthlessly professional – no, that is too dignified a word, let us substitute *commercial* – organisation. For Rolls-Royce conveyed to him that his service agreement with Bentley Motors was still in force, and that he was therefore to be considered as part of the assets that they had purchased, 'together' as he put it, 'with the office furniture'. He also learned, which must have been even more distressing, that Rolls-Royce had no intention of pursuing the development of his 8-litre car or indeed any of his others

It was a shrewd manoeuvre on the part of Rolls-Royce, though it will be perpetually lamented by all those who admire the man Bentley and his work, by all those who recall with similar admiration the superb feats of engineering which glorified the name of Napier, and indeed by all those who value the variety and vigour that once distinguished the British automobile industry. For Rolls-Royce it effectively eliminated competition from the company's two greatest British rivals. That shrewd man of affairs Claude Johnson would doubtless have approved had he been living; and the equally hard-headed new managing director Sid-

greaves, who had taken over after a two-years interregnum by Johnson's brother Basil, might well have smiled at the thought that the Rolls-Royce engineering staff now included not only two men of exceptional ability and authority (Rowledge and Elliot) who had come from the now doomed Napier Company, but also the man who in the brief life of Bentley Motors Limited had done as much to enhance the reputation of British automotive engineering abroad as Rolls-Royce had done in a considerably longer time.

Bentley's task with his new masters was to produce a well-mannered sporting car derived from the 20/25 horsepower Rolls-Royce. The chassis of this had earned his approval after he had tested it at Brooklands, and after some dithering over alternative engines it was decided that modification of the 20/25 engine, including raised compression ratio, crossflow manifolding and cylinder head and twin carburettors, would suffice to give the desired performance. The result was 'the silent sports car', the $3\frac{1}{2}$-litre Bentley, which those who could tell the difference between Cricklewood and Derby preferred to call the Rolls Bentley. It was a splendid car, of that there is no doubt, though in character it was neither Bentley nor Rolls-Royce. It came on the market in 1933.

That was the year in which Royce died. He had played some part in the acquisition of Bentley, though he was denied the opportunity to see the take over brought to fruition. Perhaps this did not matter a great deal: there were plenty of other and better things to his credit, and the forcefulness of his personality and philosophy were such as amply to justify all those enthusiasts who persist in calling all his cars – and even those that were built after his death – simply by the name Royce. His was the conviction that only the best was good enough, his the gift for recognising what was best. When he died on 22nd April 1933 he left a successor but not a replacement, for the criterion that every new Rolls-Royce car or component had now to meet before being put into production was whether it would have met with Royce's approval. Only one thing was allowed to change: the initials RR that appear as a monogram on the company's badge were changed in colour from red to black – and according to some authorities, the real reason for this was aesthetic. Under the bonnet, engine finish was black and aluminium; and it was urged that the badge should relate to this rather than recall the days of brass and copper plumbing. It could have been the true reason for the change; was sorrow for the passing of Royce then the occasion for the change, or was it a curious coincidence? The whole truth turns out to be rather different and more convincing than either of these explanations, of which one seems too fortuitous and the other too fatuous. It turns, nevertheless, on a question of aesthetic sensibilities: for the red of the original badge had been seen to clash with the colouring of many bodies; and after some initial resistance

to the idea of change, Royce had finally agreed to the substitution of perfectly neutral colours for the badge so that nothing in the Rolls-Royce part of the vehicle should sort ill with any of its other elements. Thus the badge was neutralised into black and silver, Royce's final decision being almost literally so, for he made it one month before his death. It was to be more than a month before any car could be delivered with the revised badge; and the obvious conclusions were drawn. Mozart, it will be remembered, believed he was writing his own Requiem Mass; did it likewise fall to Royce to mourn his own death?

Although the company and its devotees often insist that the death of Royce made no difference to the products,

Probably the Parisian 'carrossiers' produced the best results on the Phantom 2. The Countess Dorothy di Frasso's Darrin-bodied car, seen here in the streets of New York, epitomises their choicest work

When the RR radiator was pushed forward on the Phantom 3, it unbalanced existing body styles

there are some grounds for judging the Phantom 3, which appeared in 1936, as not only the last of the great classical cars but also in some ways the first of the modern ones. Most compelling of these features was the independent front suspension, contrived as a four-bar linkage and fashioned after the manner of General Motors, a firm to whom Rolls-Royce have often looked for technical leads. Apart from this suspension, the most outstanding feature of the Phantom 3 was its engine, a V12 which was dimensionally a pair of 20/25 engines on a common crankcase and shaft. This made the capacity 7,340 cm^3 and the RAC rating 50.7hp, though the output was 165bhp at 3,000 rev/min and later grew with the adoption of four-port cylinder heads in 1938 to about 180. This was equivalent to a bmep of 105 lb/in^2, but neither the company nor the customers were likely to care over-

much: what mattered, as ever, was that the bmep and torque were extremely high at very low engine speed, so that the Phantom 3 retained the top gear flexibility so eagerly sought by drivers of the big cars.

There were other interesting new refinements in the engine. In the ignition system, for example, the magneto had disappeared and now there were two separate coil ignition sets. The valves were all operated by a single camshaft mounted in the V of the crankcase and, although the push-rod and rocker mechanism was conventional, the tappets were of a new zero-lash type, hydraulically adjusted so as to maintain contact and silence throughout all ranges of speed and temperature. The Americans had done it earlier, and so had Napier in their aero engines, but so far as British cars were concerned, the P3 was the first with hydraulic tappets, and the engine was undoubtedly very quiet indeed. It was also of course free at long last from the pestilential torsional flutter problems that inevitably beset the in-line six configuration to which Rolls-Royce had previously been addicted. It is not improbable that this consideration weighed as much with Rolls-Royce as did the reason that they gave for adopting the V12, namely that it enabled the engine to be made shorter and thus to save space. It is true that the wheelbase of the P3 was eight inches less than that of the P2 while there was more space for bodywork; but it was not only the shortened engine that made this possible, but also the adoption of independent front suspension, accompanied by the characteristic displacement forward of the engine and radiator. The tendency of succeeding models to grow taller in the bonnet, evident since the days of the Silver Ghost, had not yet run its course; but the radiator of the P3 seemed to tower higher than ever, looking rather more gross not only because of its height but also because it was set further forward. It was not

easy for the established coachbuilders to adapt their styles to this change of proportion, and many of the bodies which clothed the P3 looked ungainly. The proportions were further altered subtly by the reduction in wheel diameter to 18 inches, where the P2 had wheels of 20 or 19 inches diameter (apart from the 17 inch wheels of the last Continental models).

The P3 was therefore not a pretty car, and seldom was it handsome. In its behaviour, though, it was one of the very best large luxury cars of its time and one of the best Rolls-Royce models. It proved to have a considerably higher cornering power than the earlier Phantoms and of course it was much faster – which meant more to prospective and actual owners than

The Phantom 3 was always imposing, if often ugly. One of the least offensive bodies for it was this Park Ward sedanca de ville

And who minds a little austerity when in a Rolls-Royce (above) dicky-seat for the occasional extra passenger and (below) a Weymann fabric 20/25

Above : This Brewster bodied Springfield Phantom 1 interior appears to offer more comfort than (below) Hooper's counterpart on a Phantom 3 chassis

Sir Arthur Sidgreaves, who became managing director after the Johnson era

any amount of brake horsepower or bmep figures. If not impossibly bodied it would do 95; later cars would do a genuine 100mph, and the last thirty or so cars which had overdrive gearing could reach a still higher speed. More to the point was the acceleration, often described in the sycophantic flattery to which the motoring press of the day was addicted as 'like that of a racing car' or at least 'enough to put the best sports car to shame'.

This of course is arrant nonsense. The better racing cars of 1937 could accelerate from standstill to 100mph in about ten seconds, reaching 60mph in about four seconds. This may be an extreme example, but it would not be unreasonable to consider the straight-eight Hudson-engined Brough Superior car which could reach 60mph in ten seconds from a standing start. The Phantom 3 took about sixteen seconds for the 0 to 60 dash, which was not as good as everyone pretended but nevertheless a good deal quicker than most people were accustomed to. Perhaps more important was that the acceleration in top gear from 20 to 40mph was quicker than from 30 to 50,

and from 10 to 30mph it was quicker still, showing that if Rolls-Royce wanted to ensure a high bmep at low revs they certainly knew how to get it.

Earlier in these pages it was suggested that the P3 was an unusual amalgam of the modern and the classical. Certainly it had some endearing old-fashioned features. For example the gearbox was again separate from the engine, both components being separately mounted. This change not only allowed a particularly massive cruciform cross-member to be set well forward on the chassis, so that the crux came between engine and gearbox, but also by bringing the gearbox further aft improved the weight distribution a little, shortened the propeller shaft and put the right-hand gear lever in just the right place – alongside the seat, where a hand might naturally fall for it, instead of being up ahead of the driver's knee and constituting a navigational hazard whenever he got in or out of the car. This apart, it was really a rather modern gearbox, for there was now synchromesh on second gear as well as on third and fourth, and the action was quite delightful. So was that of the steering, which was remarkably light considering the amount of weight on the front wheels, and it still had the old-fashioned virtue of reasonably high gearing, needing just three turns of the hand wheel to go from lock to lock – though the turning circle thus encompassed measured forty-eight feet in diameter so that the effective gearing was not as high as all that.

At any rate, what with the great power, inordinate flexibility, sweet steering and gorgeous gearbox, the Phantom 3 was a delightful car. Indeed its natal 1936 may be considered a vintage year, for shortly after the introduction of the P3 there was revealed a new version of the baby Rolls. The engine of this had been bored out yet again to $3\frac{1}{2}$ inches, giving it a capacity of $4\frac{1}{4}$ litres. Thus the 20/25 became the 25/30, an exquisite car that was beautifully balanced,

sensibly dimensioned and adequately fast. The earlier small Rolls-Royce cars had always been slower than any Rolls-Royce should be, and were often criticised for their want of power; the 25/30 certainly had no excess of it but was fast enough not to be a source of embarrassment. It would do a genuine eighty unless overbodied, and handled gracefully. The same applied *mutatis mutandis* to the 4¼-litre Bentley which was its sporting equivalent; but at least the Bentley did last for three years. Lamentably the 25/30, perhaps the nicest Rolls-Royce of all, endured for only two years before giving way to modernism in the shape of the Wraith – which was tantamount to a 25/30 engine in a scaled-down P3 chassis, welded instead of being put together with fitted tapered bolts in reamed holes as had been the traditional Derby manner. Like the P3, the Wraith looked ungainly; but in any case it only lasted for a year (491 were made) before events took a turn for the worse and Rolls-Royce turned to the wars. Curiously, motor car manufacture did not come to a complete halt, for the Mark 5 Bentley, which was a sort of sporting Wraith with overdrive gearbox and beautifully close ratios, fifteen-inch wheels and in most cases a particularly handsome and convincing saloon body by Park Ward, was in production from 1939 until 1941. This bald statement might unsupported give an altogether erroneous impression of the scale of the affair, but fewer than twenty cars were actually built.

The silent sports-car: a Rolls-Royce cocktail mixed by Bentley

One or two other oddities and specials were produced during the war. There was the notorious Scalded Cat, for example, fitted with one of the first of the straight-eight overhead-inlet side-exhaust engines of the B series and evidently rather low geared since its maximum speed in neutral conditions was 101.5mph only, while it could climb Porlock Hill in top gear. The same engine incidentally had powered a Rolls-Royce limousine prototype called Big Bertha, which was to find its expression in a limited production run of the Phantom 4 after the war. However, these were mere prototypes such as any manufacturer will toy with from time to time, eventually sweeping them under the carpet or putting them under the hammer. For all practical purposes the manufacture of Rolls-Royce cars finished when the war started, as was only right and proper. Virtually the same applied to Bentley – and in any case W O Bentley himself had some time earlier managed to free himself of his bondage and had gone to Lagonda, where he first improved and developed the 4½ litre LG 45 and LG 6 cars and then designed and saw put into production (and raced, most impressively at Le Mans) the Lagonda V12, which he and many others consider the best thing he ever did. Alas, most people never knew that he was concerned with it, for Rolls-Royce would not permit Bentley's name to be used in any way.

A rare picture of a unique car: the original Bentley Corniche. Not to be confused with the Embiricos and Hay cars which later carried the name, the real Corniche was destroyed by a bomb at Dunkirk

TOWARDS THE WAR TO END ALL HOPE

By the time the Great War ended in November 1918, Rolls-Royce had a bigger version of the Eagle in production for the Handley Page V/1500-bomber. It had been designed in a tremendous hurry, and this fact as much as Rolls-Royce conservatism was responsible for the fact that this big new V12, known as the Condor, was little more than a scaled-up version of the Eagle. Only in two respects were the engines significantly different: the connecting rods were of knife and fork pattern instead of being paired as master and articulated slave, and the big combustion chambers now housed four valves (with the valve gear altered correspondingly) instead of two. Otherwise it was just another Eagle, grossed up to a capacity of 35 litres and an output of 600 horsepower. It was thus beginning to rival the most powerful foreign engine, and was certainly far bigger and lustier than anything else in Britain. But, with the end of the war, Rolls-Royce could see no further use for it.

Indeed they wanted nothing more to do with the aero engine business, being far too busy making Silver Ghosts for the flourishing car market. The aviation department was reduced to a shadow of its former self, as happened in most other aero engine factories where the effects of a sud-

The RR-powered Vimy made history in 1919 when it was the first aircraft to cross the Atlantic non-stop

denly diminished market were aggravated by the vast stocks of war surplus engines available at nominal or even derisory prices. In fact the Rolls-Royce aviation department spent two years doing nothing but overhauling engines that had been built during the war.

Meanwhile their former rivals Napier were going ahead with the development and marketing of their broad-arrow 12 cylinder Lion aero engine, designed by the brilliant A J Rowledge. By 1921 the Lion was an engine of outstanding merit, already distinguished by successes in racing, already recognised as exemplary in reliability, and already showing considerable scope for development to even greater levels of performance. By contrast the Condor was almost forgotten, an underprivileged under-developed heavy lump, not yet blessed with any reliability, and already obsolete in its costruction which still recalled the practices of a decade earlier.

What had seemed to Rolls-Royce not to matter in 1919 became a matter of some moment in 1921. The car market was not doing at all well, and the profits that could be made on a typical government contract for aero engine development began to seem a great deal more enticing.

One must not censure Rolls-Royce too strictly for the attitude they took in 1919, because there was very little incentive for them to pursue aero engine development. The Great War had been the war to end all wars, after all, and Rolls-Royce experience of aviation had been in a strictly military context. Civil aviation was still faltering and far from being a convincing entity, so quantity orders for engines were practically non-existent. In any case where was the money to come from? The total resources of Government for engine development contracts were at best only about £200,000 per year, sometimes nearer £100,000. Allowing this to be spread over a reasonable number of jobs (the hedging of bets was a time-honoured government practice) this meant that

even a large development contract would be worth no more than, say, £30,000. Compared with the profit to be made from the sales of the Silver Ghost, especially with the new American factory at Springfield getting under way, such sums were almost beneath contempt. Government asked Rolls-Royce to continue development of the Condor at government expense, but Claude Johnson flatly refused.

By 1921, with the post-war depression effective and the bottom out of the luxury car market, Rolls-Royce looked more kindly upon the aero engine business. By this time, however it was impossible for them to get back into it on their own resources: two years of neglect had left them and their Condor outstripped by Napier and their Lion. All that the company could do was to go cap in hand to the Air Ministry and ask for any work that happened to be going.

They got their answer from Lieutenant-Colonel Fell, the assistant director for engine design and research: Rolls-Royce should develop the Condor to an output of 650 horsepower and improve its reliability Soon the company was given a contract for the production of about 200 engines, though there were at the time no aircraft ready to accommodate them. Maybe, as was to happen so many times in the future, Rolls-Royce were simply being cosseted through a difficult stage by Government, who knew that the time would come when the qualities of Rolls-Royce engineering would be a valuable asset. Perhaps in this particular instance the Air Ministry judged that by the time the Condor had been made good, suitable aircraft for it would be found. Doubtless the Napier Lion would fit them equally well, but doubtless it was unwise to put all their eggs in one basket.

As it happened, that same year Rolls-Royce made another acquisition that must have been of as great value to them as this precious government contract. They acquired the services of A J Rowledge, the designer of the

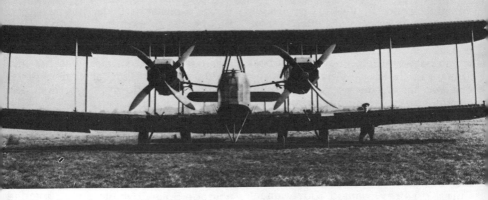

Lion, who had just left Napier after some serious disagreement with their management. He was promptly put in charge of Rolls-Royce aviation work at Derby. Rowledge was a brilliant man about whom too little has been recorded, though he was probably the greatest engineer in the service of the company at any time in its history. He was already forty-five when he joined Rolls-Royce, a tall slim greying man who always wore, as he did throughout his life (he died in 1957 after retiring in 1945), a stiff high single collar which gave him an air of considerable if conservative distinction in contrast to the sartorial sloppiness of Royce.

To begin with, Rowledge was set to work on the Condor and he made the best of a bad job, redesigning it, raising the output to the desired figure, and improving it in many ways. Work staggered on with the Condor being taken through five different forms before eventually Government told Rolls-Royce to stop work on it: this was in 1925, by which time it was recognised by maker and buyer alike that the Condor was useless, an expensive liability. One of the factors effecting Government's decision was the pains taken by Rolls-Royce to convince them that no other firm could possibly produce the Condor – to which the response was that in that case some other engines should be developed which would be less difficult to make! In any case it was clearly an outdated engine, and in the pre-

Torsional flutter of the crankshaft inhibited the operation of the Rolls-Royce Eagle V12 engines which powered the Vickers Vimy

vious year Royce himself had conducted some studies from which he had concluded that he should develop a water-cooled engine of monobloc construction, streamlined, compact and entirely new.

What prompted this change of heart was an American engine that had been breathtakingly successful since its appearance in 1922. This was the justly famous Curtiss D12, which took the world of high-speed aviation by storm. Royce reckoned that to remain competitive he should design a 16-cylinder engine of X configuration with four banks of four cylinders each being of monobloc construction, supercharged by a gear-driven compressor of the type that the Air Ministry were encouraging Bristol and Armstrong-Siddeley to develop. In January 1925 he persuaded the Air Ministry into backing the design and development of this engine, which was again called the Eagle. By the middle of the following year the Eagle 16 was giving 500 horsepower; and there it stopped.

Something else had turned up. Over in America, Curtiss had granted a manufacturing licence for the Fairey Aviation Company to manufacture the V12 in England. A two-seater military biplane was promptly designed around it by C R Fairey as a purely private venture, financed out of the profits his firm were making from building their 3F biplane for the government – and this new aircraft, christened the Fox, would outperform the newest and best fighters in the Royal Air Force. Only one was faster, the Hawker Hornbill, which never went into production because it was powered by that crude monstrosity the Condor – and why bother with a 700 horsepower engine of monstrous antiquity when the same performance could be achieved with the beautiful little 400 horsepower Curtiss? Fairey wanted Government to back him in producing V12s; but Government rebuffed him, reckoning that they had quite enough engine manufacturers already. They liked the Fox but it had to have a British engine, and that engine had to be built by one of the established firms. The establishment consisted of Armstrong Siddeley and Bristol, who were already busily engaged on air-cooled radials, of Napier who were convinced that the Lion would go on for ever and ever and make a fortune in the process so that they wanted nothing to do with any others, and Rolls-Royce who were not exactly inundated with business at the time. It was accordingly to Rolls-Royce that the Air Ministry went, with a Curtiss D12 under one arm and a contract under the other. In July 1925 Royce and his staff began the design of the Falcon X which later became known as the F and finally as the Kestrel. The work on the Eagle 16 continued, in accordance with the long established policy that anything that Rolls-Royce began had to be made to work; but once it had proved that it would work; it was dropped.

Work on the Kestrel was more important and more rewarding. It was about the same size as the Curtiss, actually $21\frac{1}{4}$ litres, but it had a two-sided centrifugal supercharger gear-driven like that of the Eagle 16, it had separate cylinder heads, and it had no reduction gears for its airscrew drive. All three of these features proved to be bad, but with Rowledge on hand to correct Royce's mistakes it did not take long before the necessary improvements were in hand. The first experimental Kestrel was run early in 1926, a geared unsupercharged version was put into production in 1927, and then Rolls-Royce settled down to sort out the problem of supercharging.

They were not altogether sure they could afford it, but Government gave various assurances (such as promising Fairey the new engine, though this promise was observed to the letter rather than in the spirit) so as to encourage Rolls-Royce to get on with the work using their own money pending the availability of government funds.

The Air Ministry also cajoled Rolls-Royce into taking on to their staff a man named Ellor. It just so happened that Ellor was a supercharging genius, having been responsible for all the pioneering work done on forced induction at the Royal Aircraft Establishment. Recognising his value, an American company had dangled large bags of gold before him, but Government knew his value too and did not want to see him go – so they dropped a hint to Rolls-Royce, who for once were ready to take a hint and hired him. It was not long before Ellor had given Rolls-Royce a blower of outstanding efficiency for the Kestrel, and in May 1928 the supercharged engine was in production in two forms, a highly boosted version rated for 13,000 feet at 520hp and the other for 2,000 feet at 580hp, and neither weighing much more than 900lbs.

Ellor was one of those rare men who constitute a challenge to the commonly held theory that nobody is indispensable. He was a specialist of such incontestable superiority that any serious aero engine firm would give anything to secure his services. What he did was to introduce an awareness of aerodynamics, such as was to stand

R for Racing, for Royce, for Rowledge – the R engine on a dynomometer stand displays its huge supercharger

the company in very good stead through all the generations of engine upon which they subsequently embarked. Nor was this limited only to the interior aerodynamics of the supercharger itself: before long the Kestrel was given a ramming air intake which increased the maximum speed of the test aircraft by nearly 10mph, and by 1928 the Kestrel was established and becoming famous. The first batch of unblown ones were despatched to Fairey's for two squadrons of Fox aircraft – and after that, all the others went to Hawker for the Hart, the Fury, and their sundry beautiful derivatives.

Even before this it was clear to Rolls-Royce and to others that the Kestrel would not satisfy the probable future requirements of Government. A larger engine, albeit of similar conception, was bound to be wanted. There was not much future now for the Lion, and there never had been any for the Condor; so on 19th June 1927 Rolls-Royce began work on a scaled-up version of the supercharged Kestrel calculated to have an even bigger capacity than the Condor. Its bore and stroke were 6 and 6.6 inches, making 36.7 litres *in toto*, and thirteen months later the first prototype was developing 925 horsepower at sea level. The idea was that it would be used in big flying boats, but it was never a success and fewer than fifty production examples were sold.

Nevertheless the Buzzard, as it was called, came in handy: for in 1928 the British Government had finally made up its mind, after ages spent in dithering, that Britain should be properly represented in the 1929 Schneider Trophy race in which the competing nations submitted teams of three single-seater floatplanes which had to undergo various trials of seaworthiness and then race over a triangular course. Several times in the past the British had either won gloriously or failed ignominiously, the aircraft being usually powered by the noble Napier Lion; but competition had been getting very fierce of late, and Government had been

losing patience with Napier, who persisted on going their own way and not doing what Government wanted them to do. Perhaps they should have known better, seeing that Government were paying them. At any rate, late in 1928 the Air Ministry approached Rolls-Royce with a view to getting something newer and better than the Lion.

They got an unwelcoming reception: Rolls-Royce did not approve of racing in any form or for any purpose, for there is too great an element of chance involved in it and the exposure to adverse publicity is proportionately great. Rolls-Royce were in fact quite right to take this attitude; but they recognised that the customer is always right, and in the aero engine business

they only had one customer. So when Major Bulman of the Air Ministry had finished telling them how good they were and how desirable a Schneider Trophy victory was – not to mention reminding them that the Air Ministry could be long in memory and tight in fist if it so chose – Rolls-Royce toed the line. Henry Royce himself was convinced that they could do what was required, and bearing in mind that the requirement was for 1,800hp it must have been a shattering display of confidence, since he promised to obtain it from the Buzzard engine whose prototype, only a few months old, gave barely half this amount.

Clearly Royce was putting his faith in Ellor, for the principle means at his disposal for doubling the power output

Britain's 1929 Schneider Trophy winner, the R-engined Supermarine S6

of the Buzzard was an entirely new supercharger, designed to be as large as possible, its diameter being determined by the cross-sectional shape of the fuselage of the Supermarine S6 seaplane into which the engine was to be fitted. This allowed the supercharger to be very large in diameter, but if sufficient airflow were to be achieved the impellor would still have to be two-sided. Rolls-Royce had already built blowers of this type, though they had not been good ones; but now with Ellor on hand the faults were eradicated. Inlet manifold pressure was raised to nearly one atmosphere above ambient and this, combined with the compression ratio of 6:1 inside the cylinders, led to a power output of no less than 1,900hp at 2,500 rev/min, equivalent to a bmep of 225lb/in^2. Not all of this was due to the super-charging, for the ramming air intake that had been tried on the Kestrel was used as well, being itself worth 250hp at 350mph.

Development of the engine, known as the R, was entrusted to Rowledge. At his direction most of the structure and the exterior of the engine was revised, either to strengthen it to sustain the increased loadings or to adapt it to the aerodynamic requirements of the air-frame. The work was done very fast, but it was done with great punctilio, with the result that by May 1929 one of the development engines (there were at least six) was already making en-durance runs on the dynamometer. By August the promised figure of 1,800hp could be maintained for an hour, but in the intervening months there were difficulties symptomised by tightening up and loss of power after about twenty minutes. The cure was prescribed by F R Banks of the Associated Ethyl Company (he later became an RAF Air Commodore and Director of Aero Engine Production) who recognised the unsuitability of the pure benzole in the fuel that had been used and recom-mended a mixture of 78 percent ben-zole, 22 percent Rumanian petrol and a dash of tetraethyl lead. By the time the race took place in September 1929 the R was ready with 1,900hp, yet weighing only 1,530 lb.

By the standards of its time the R was incredible and the specific weight was respectable. In terms of ratio of power to frontal area (which was more impor-tant to the realisation of high airspeeds) there was simply nothing to compare with it. Its only apparent failings were its tremendous thirst: its specific fuel consumption was nearly as bad as that of the original Eagle, equivalent to more than 3½ gallons a minute or some-thing like 160 gallons in the course of the race, and oil consumption amounted to 10 gallons an hour, ten times worse than the Eagle although not too bad by racing standards.

Racing standards somehow did not seem appropriate to a Rolls-Royce engine, and the 1929 R was typical of the company: there was nothing much about the design that was original or even noteworthy but the development work was quite fantastic. The fact that it had been done in so little time strained the bounds of credibility, and the only thing that stopped it all seeming a miracle was the simple fact that in the first place Royce had said that it could be done.

What he said in January 1931 when it was decided again that Britain should take part in the Schneider Trophy contest is not known. We need not doubt that his usual coarse and vulgar vocabulary was not wanting in expres-siveness; but he must have seen how greatly the reputation of Rolls-Royce had been enhanced by the British success in 1929, when the R-engined Supermarine seaplane won the race and then established a new world speed record by the great margin of 50mph. But on that occasion he had been given eleven months to produce a raceworthy engine; this time he had only eight. Government had been reluctant to support the event, due to the shortage of money and a disinclination to offend large numbers of unemployed by spending money on aeroplane races. It was only because Lady Houston recognised the importance to Britain of maintaining an international reputation that the decision was eventually taken to go ahead, on the security of her cheque for £100,000; and once again Rolls-Royce were asked to produce a race-winning engine. In some ways this was a greater challenge than in 1929, for the Italians were known to be working on new engines and aircraft of revolutionary design and quite

Sir Henry Royce chats in the stiff Calshot breeze to the Schneider Trophy pilots of the RAF High Speed Flight

staggering power, whereas Supermarine could do no better than revise the 1929 S6 airframe. With so little scope for manoeuvre and so little time for thought, the only possible course was to get as much power out of the R as they could and hope that this would be enough.

The means of doing so involved higher revs and even more supercharge. The blower was run faster, the air intake increased in size, and the result was a boost of 18lb/in^2, again with the ram intake which was worth 10 percent and still with the original 6:1 compression ratio. A new fuel was devised consisting of 70 percent benzole, 20 percent Californian petrol and 10 percent methanol plus lead, and with all these the design power rose to 2,350hp. Rolls-Royce said that they would pass the engine for racing when it could maintain this continuously for one hour, but it was to be a long time before that happy day; a relatively long time that is, although considering that the whole programme had to be completed in less than nine months, it was really amazingly brief. Considering the increased output and the higher inertia loads involved, Rowledge and his team found it necessary to change practically every stressed part of the engine: the blade and fork connecting rods were replaced by articulated pairs, the crankshaft had to be modified (centrifugal and inertia forces totalled no less than nine tons on the centre mainbearing), all sorts of bearing materials were tried and sodium cooled exhaust valves were used for the first time on any Rolls-Royce engine, though Heron had introduced them ten years earlier in America. Most significantly, many bronze and steel components were replaced by aluminium alloy forgings, the new materials being developed by Rolls-Royce themselves as part of their Hiduminium series which are still current and respected. They helped to keep the total weight of the engine down to 1,640 lb and helped it to hold together when eventually on 3rd August 1931 an R engine gave

2,360 hp for fifty-eight minutes. This was not an hour, and Rolls-Royce were true to their word. Compared with the mere twenty minutes that the engine would last in April or the half-hour that it might give in July, it was near enough for nobody to complain, but Rolls-Royce were having no half measures. Nine days later they did what they set out to do, a one-hour run at 2,350hp.

Now the problems of installation began. The engine might work on the dynamometer, but in the aircraft new difficulties appeared. Water was lost from the cooling system; oil exuded from every pore. The ten gallons per hour rate of oil consumption that had not seemed unreasonable in 1929 now seemed downright frugal: the new R was getting through fifty gallons an hour, more than the oil tank capacity of the aircraft would allow. On one occasion when the engine was run in the test house for twenty-five minutes it used twenty-seven gallons of oil, flinging the stuff around so that the interior of the test house and everything and everybody that it contained was absolutely glistening with the stuff. The oil was of course pure castor, so that the bodies involved were more than emotionally upset by the problem, but it was the intellectual and mechanical challenge of a rate of consumption equivalent to 112 gallons an hour that kept them going, so-to-speak. Weeks of intensive work were devoted to curing the oil consumption problem, which seemed basically to be associated with problems of breathing and piston ring blow-by as is usually the case with high oil consumption. Knife-edged scraper rings were developed for the pistons, the scavenging system was modified, new crankcase breathers were designed, and a big new sump was shaped to fit so closely inside the engine cowling that its expansion by a mere 0.15 inch when hot gave the engineers serious worries. That deep sump made a big difference to the oil temperature rise, oil going into the engine at about 80 degrees

entigrade and coming out at 140. One
way and another they reduced the
oil consumption to fourteen gallons an
hour, though it took them a long time
before they could measure this ac-
curately, the difficulties created by the
complicated plumbing of the aircraft
being such that on one occasion more
oil was drained out of the system than
calculations suggested could ever have
been put into it.

When race day came and the foreign
opposition did not, everybody relaxed.
It would be a walkover win for Great
Britain. However, the Royal Air Force
does not content itself with that sort of
spirit, and Flight-Lieutenant Boothman
of the High Speed Flight did not hang
around when he set out in the S6B. He
could have cruised around gently and
cossetted the engine, just so as to make
sure that Britain might win; but this had
to be a famous victory, since it would
give Britain the hat trick and the trophy
in perpetuity according to the rules.
Better to be a hare than a tortoise;
Boothman flew around the course at a
new record speed, averaging over
340mph. As he flew on, the engine let
out a long trail of black smoke from its
exhaust, the smoke increasing as time
went on – the knife edge of the scraper
rings was gradually being blunted.
Then the water temperature began to
rise and it was not only the smoke that
was black. Boothman's response to this
was to throttle back from his full-bore
3,200 rev/min to 3,100, and after thirty
minutes of caning the R brought the
Schneider Trophy home for good. A
few minutes later the other S6B was
taken out by that great pilot then Flight-
Lieutenant Stainforth to attack the
world's speed record, succeeding at
over 379mph.

A fortnight later he was doing it
again, for now Rolls-Royce could give
him even more power. A new fuel
blend containing no petrol but co-
taining acetone and more lead than
before allowed an uprating to 2,530hp,
to absorb which a new airscrew was
specially built. Even then the R was not
fully extended, for it did an endurance

run of one hour on the dynomometer at
3,400 rev/min, developing 2,783hp.

It was a great engine. It golloped its
fuel at 0.85 lb/hph, it burned up or
spewed out an undisclosed quantity of
oil, and it gave Stainforth the world's
speed record at 407.5mph, breaking the
400mph figure for the first time. Nor was
that the end of its competitive career: it
became sought after as a power unit for
contenders for the land speed record:
Malcolm Campbell's series of Blue-
birds, once Lionised, now used R power
to take the land speed record in 1933 at
272mph, in 1935 at 276mph, and again
in that same year at 301mph. On water,
Segrave's Miss England II achieved a
water speed record of 98.76mph in 1930
with the help of two R engines, and the
same craft piloted by Kaye Don did
103mph and then 110mph in 1931. Miss
England III, similarly powered, did
nearly 120mph in 1932; then in 1937
Malcolm Campbell took over with his
Bluebird boat relying on one R engine
to do 129.5mph, which he raised to
nearly 131mph in 1938 and 142mph
in 1939. Thus at one time the R was
the fastest on land, on water and in
the air, though the airspeed record was
taken from Britain by the Fiat-engined
MC72 seaplane in 1933. When Messerschmitt concluded a bout of record
breaking by setting the world speed-
record at 469mph in 1939 they did so
with the help of a Daimler-Benz engine
developing 2,770hp. Though it was not
Rolls-Royce's fault if Britain did not
retain the air record, there was no
question of the R being anything but
an exceptional engine, one of the most
resplendent jewels in the Rolls-Royce
crown.

Of course, since it was a racing
engine it was atypical of Rolls-Royce
and for this reason it had only a limited
life. The official figure was five hours
between overhauls, but when after the
elapse of this time it was returned to
Derby for stripping it was usually
found capable of another ten hours
running. In the 1940s engines of comparable size and power would be run
for hundreds of hours between over-

hauls; but back in 1931 when fuels, supercharging, lubrication and metal-· lurgy were even more imperfectly understood than now, the standards set by Rolls-Royce with the R were such as other engine manufacturers could barely hope to follow.

Most contemporary references to the success of the engine amounted to little more than uncritical adulation, and this is not really to be wondered at. Nevertheless the journal *Aircraft Engineering* gave a sober assessment of the story in 1932. 'It strikes us as being pre-eminently a story of patience. Standing out all through is a painstaking attention to small details, combined with a truly scientific examination of every difficulty and problem as it arose, in order to discover the cause of it. The care

that had been taken in such matters a checking the moisture content of th fuel to ensure its suitability, and arriv ing at the best method of filling th water and fuel systems, give a extraordinarily vivid picture of patience that must at times have re quired almost superhuman control if were not to break down.'

This is the sort of thing that is under stood by the expression 'Rolls-Royc engineering'; and if the results of suc an approach were of such unques able merit, who is to say that Rolls-Royc engineering is at fault ? The R provide a good example, though by no mean the last or even the most convincing, c the value of Rolls-Royce developmen work. It is perhaps difficult to suppres concern about the quality of the basi

design if so much development should be necessary; but the speed with which it was all done was nothing short of fantastic, and perhaps there could be little wrong with the basic design if it could be developed so far in so short a time.

We are forced to reconsider this judgement by the example of the Merlin, the most famous engine of them all and the one that is most popularly held to exemplify the potential results that can be achieved by development in Rolls-Royce style. The Merlin came later, was less powerful, gave far more trouble and took years to get right, not just months. It is hard to see why it should have been so recalcitrant when the Buzzard was capable of such rapid development into a world beater,

Miss England 2, Lord Wakefield's boat, had two R engines. In her, Sir Henry Segrave took the world speed record for boats from Miss America 7 at 98.76mph in 1930, and Kaye Don took it from Miss America 8 at 103.49mph in 1931, later raising it to 110.81mph

especially considering that both grew out of the Kestrel. There is only one really significant difference in the circumstances attaching to these respective engines, and it is hard to avoid the conclusion that it must be a particularly telling difference: the R was developed by Royce and Rowledge, the Merlin under Hives and Elliot.

Or was the essential difference that

103

Miss England 3 also had two Rs, and took the water speed record from Miss America 9 in 1932 at 119.81mph

which exists between a racing engine and a military one? By the time the Merlin was expected to go into service, standards of aero engine durability had risen considerably, mainly due to the work of Bristol, Wright and Pratt & Whitney in the development of large air-cooled radial engines. The Rolls-Royce Merlin was designed to be powerful rather than to be economical, and it is in the nature of such engines to wear themselves out relatively quickly. As we shall see, the Merlin had great difficulty in getting through its hundred-hour type test, and at one stage a little semi-official cheating had to be done in order to get the thing into production. Years later when the Second World War was over and Rolls-Royce were trying to get the Merlin into the civil aviation market, they had to do a tremendous amount of work on it in order to make its overhaul life even tolerable by commercial standards. Yet the Merlin was a great engine, from an historical point of view probably the greatest. What made it so? Some commentators have avowed that the Daimler-Benz engines, for example, were better designed; others have suggested that certain Napiers and possibly Bristols were better made; but nobody would ever suggest that any piston engine had ever been more thoroughly and doggedly developed than the Merlin.

So we must again consider the merit of development. It is easy to argue that it is at best a poor, expensive and time-consuming substitute for good design. Of all the jibes flung at Rolls-Royce over the years, the one that is best known and has stuck is that of the late L H

The last of Sir Malcolm Campbell's 'Bluebird' cars, this R-engined 1935 version was the first to raise the land speed record above 300mph

Two great engineers both came from Napier A J Rowledge . . .

Pomeroy, who said that the Rolls-Royce represented 'the triumph of workmanship over design'. Did Rolls-Royce place too much reliance on their ability to rectify errors that other manufacturers would be more careful to avoid in the first place? And if they did, were they perhaps right to do so, being blessed with a staff of gifted development engineers who were there to be exploited? Or was it a fault of the system by which they were financed by Government, on terms which encouraged them to work this way, producing hardware for which they would be paid and then doing work on it for which they would be paid more, rather than doing a lot of hard preliminary thinking whose value no accountant could assess?

According to Rolls-Royce publicity material, this last reason could not have been valid because the Merlin originated as a private venture, conceived and financed by the company itself without government assistance. Like so many other statements issued from time to time by the fearsomely efficient Rolls-Royce propaganda machine, it needs to be treated guardedly as a sort of half truth. Certainly it was the

company which got the idea, about th middle of 1932, that future fighter should have a larger engine than th Kestrel, which had been brought ou five years before and was beginnin to be thought outgrown. The Buzzar was too large and heavy for it to b suitable for an interceptor, and so the concluded that what was wanted was a engine that was an almost exact scale-u of the Kestrel, twenty percent greater i capacity, intended to yield about 750hp Equally certainly, although the Ai Ministry was kept fully informed of th company's intention to begin th development and approved fully of th plan, no funds were available at th time to support it. However, it is know that the company had the support i spirit of the Ministry, for it was in cor sultation with them that the compan decided to build the engine for inverte installation, so as to give the pilot bette visibility amongst other reasons. A most certainly it was common know ledge throughout the industry that th Air Ministry had plans for a ne generation of fighters, for the Napie firm embarked at about the same tim on its own series of high-power ultra compact engines. Furthermore Faire were still trying to get into the aer engine business and in late 1929 o early 1930 an employee of the Ai Ministry, Graham Forsythe, went t Fairey and designed an engine of abou the same size as the Merlin. It was water-cooled V12 called (perhaps ur fortunately) the Fairey Prince, and it wa built, run and flown at private expense The government would still not cor sider Fairey as an engine builder (the refused again later when Fairey pro posed an H-type engine) but it i stretching coincidence a bit to thin that Fairey and Forsythe had no notio of the Ministry's future plans.

As it happened, the first mock-up o the inverted Rolls-Royce engine wa given a hostile reception by the ai frame manufacturers when they saw towards the end of 1932, and they in sisted that the engine be built for up right operation. They were probabl wrong to do so, but Rolls-Royce toed the line and began detailed designing early in 1933. Drawings were issued in April of that year, but on the 22nd of that month Sir Henry Royce died. By this time Rowledge was in poor health, so the new chief engineer was Elliot while General Manager of the company and director of all engineering policy was Hives, formerly head of the experimental department. They got the PV (private venture) 12 engine under way, and the first pair of experimental engines were built and just ready for test by October when the Air Ministry had undertaken to take over the cost of the venture. In other words it was never seriously considered as a wholly privately financed operation; Government was merely short of funds when it was begun, and anxious that work should begin, and encouraged Rolls-Royce to get on with the job in the knowledge that all development from October 1933 onwards would be directly paid for by the government under a development contract.

They might have saved themselves a lot of money if they had insisted that Rolls-Royce stick faithfully to the idea of enlarging the Kestrel. As it was, the company chose to depart from that design in some respects despite the fact that the Kestrel had by this time shown itself eminently satisfactory. As soon as the two experimental PV12 prototypes were put on test, troubles began. The double helical reduction gear broke time after time, the cylinder jackets kept cracking, and a lot of redesigning and restressing of the crankcase and cylinder structures had to be done even at this early stage. After nine months one of the prototypes passed a type test giving 625 hp at sea level, 790hp at 12,000 feet, and weighing 1,177 lb. Once this stage had been reached Elliot thought it proper to embark on a new cylinder head design to replace the separate head that was a feature of the PV12. He drew his inspiration from a cylinder head that he had designed some time before 1927 for one of the cars, pre-

A G Elliott who eventually became joint managing-director

sumably the Phantom II. This cylinder head was designed to give shortened flame travel and considerable charge turbulence, and in the two-valve form it was very successful on the car. On the Merlin it had to be adapted to accommodate four valves, and in this may lurk the reasons for its failure. Unfortunately the ramp head, as it was known, was not an immediate failure: the engine embodying it was known as the Merlin B and it gave 950hp at a simulated 11,000 feet, encouraging the retention of the ramp head on all subsequent experimental Merlins up to the F which went into production as the Merlin 1.

After the adoption of the ramp head, the next changes were mainly to simplify construction, and the Merlin C had separate crankcase and cylinder blocks for this reason. When it was ready, flight testing began and cooling systems troubles immediately appeared so that Rolls-Royce had to give up the curious composite cooling system that they had copied from the American Army (which had been playing with it since about 1923) and adopt pure ethylene glycol as a coolant. Much more serious were the troubles given

It took RR a long time to get the Merlin right, but eventually it was superb. At about the half–way stage they were making this 1,460hp version, the Merlin 20, for certain marks of Beaufighter, Defiant, Halifax, Hurricane and Lancaster

by the ramp head : local detonation was causing very bad erosion, distortion led to exhaust valve failures and cylinder heads kept cracking. A Merlin C was submitted for the civil 50-hour type test in May 1935 at a maximum rating of 1,045hp, but it failed. In December of that year a Merlin E finally passed this 50-hour civil test but in the following March it failed the 100-hour military type test. Things were beginning to look bad, and as an emergency measure it was decided to scale up the standard Kestrel head to match the Merlin and to use the same Kestrel one-piece head-and-block construction, even though the placing of the cylinders in the Merlin was too close to permit a really reliable seal

between the liner and the head. One way and another there was a real panic on, for the dangers of war were daily becoming more apparent and there was great pressure to get Merlins into production to equip the Hurricane fighters and Battle day bombers which were just due to go into production. Rolls-Royce and Government agreed that in order to keep things ticking over the Merlin 1 (the F) would be put into production right away, and that the type test regulations would be relaxed for this model to permit replacement of the valves during the test.

The first production Merlin 1 was delivered in July 1936, but not until November could it pass the type test, even taking advantage of the Ministry's special dispensation. One month before, the Merlin G with the integral Kestrel-type head had gone through its test with no trouble at all. What were they to do ?

What they did was to tell Hawker to wait for the production version of the G, the Merlin 2, and to unload the 180

Mark 1 Merlins on poor Fairey. At last, in August 1937, the Merlin 2 went into production, but soon the anticipated leakage problems arose and once again a redesign was necessary. A new block with separate head was begun in March 1938 but for many purposes it was too late. Development might proceed rapidly, as we have seen it could; but production commitments forced Rolls-Royce to persevere with the old construction until the Merlin 61 appeared in 1942. In fact Merlins with separate heads of this design were actually produced by Packard before they were produced by Rolls-Royce.

Told in this way, the story of the Merlin's formative years is almost frightening. We remember the brave words that were bandied about the Merlin during the Battle of Britain, and wonder how much of this was pure propaganda – but nobody who was around at the time could deny that the engine did all that could reasonably be asked of it, even in its then imperfect form. In fact, by the time that the Merlin 61 came along, Rolls-Royce had long passed the stage of trying to make the engine work and were simply making it work better. This was something at which they were very good, of course, and the engine went from strength to strength. All sorts of detailed modifications were made to tailor it to specific aircraft, to adapt it for particular roles, and constantly to get more power and more reliability. With the aid of improved fuels, supercharger developments went on apace, and subsequent improvements to the rating of the Merlin owe more to scientific supercharging than to anything else. By the time that Germany was launching flying bombs against Britain, the Merlin RM 17 was exploiting the latest aviation fuel to give Spitfires 2,200hp or even 2,350 hp for half an hour. Even more amazing was the fifteen minutes run achieved on the dynamometer by this engine, using the same fuel with water injection, when it gave 2,640hp at 36 lb/in^2 boost, equivalent to a bmep of 404 lb/in^2. It is difficult to find much in the history of the piston engine to compare with this achievement: the even more shattering performance of the Napier Sabre is the only thing that can put it in perspective, for there is nothing else among aero engines coming anywhere near it. Rolls-Royce's old R engine gave comparable power but was much larger and its peak bmep was commensurately lower. In the Merlin, more than in anything else they had made before, Rolls-Royce demonstrated that they were without peer in engine development. They had (and therefore exploited) an incredible ability to make things properly and to make them work.

The Merlin was such an enormous success and so widely ballyhooed that its widespread acceptance forced the abandonment of two later and larger Rolls-Royce engines, the Exe and the Vulture. The Vulture came first on the drawing board, a very large engine intended for twin-engined bombers, specifically the Avro Manchester: in capacity and in general concept though not in detail it was tantamount to two Kestrels on a common crankshaft. Testing and development began in 1937 and in that year Rolls-Royce tried to interest Hawker in it for their new fighter. Hawker, having been on the wrong end of the delays and troubles surrounding the early Merlin, were understandably reluctant to make the same mistake twice and preferred the extremely promising Napier Sabre, which annoyed Rolls-Royce no end. Nevertheless they persevered with the Vulture and by 1940 it was giving 1,800 horsepower for take-off. It was heavy, though, and its frontal area was considerable. Moreover it gave trouble, and when it went into service in Manchesters in 1941 it had to be de-rated slightly: the conrods were not safe at 3,200 rev/min (which was the rate for take-off) and the engine had therefore to be limited to 3,000. Moreover it was difficult to maintain, and in any case the bomber manufacturers had discovered that four engines were better than two; and

Proudest bearer of a Merlin engine
was the Vickers-Supermarine
Spitfire, its Mitchell-designed
airframe a descendant of the
Schneider Trophy seaplanes which
were eventually RR-engined —
though the only one to have a
cantilever wing (as the Spitfire had)
was powered by a Napier Lion

When the bulky RR Vulture engine proved a flop, the Manchester twin-engined bomber for which it was intended was redesigned to carry four Merlins and became the Lancaster

eventually most Manchesters were converted into Lancasters with four Merlins.

The Exe had the same basic configuration as the Vulture, but it was smaller and it was air-cooled and it had sleeve valves. Rolls-Royce knew that Bristol and Napier were getting along well with their sleeve valve development and that Napier in particular were getting prodigious power outputs, as Sir Harry Ricardo had forecast some time earlier. However, the Exe was dropped soon after its first test flight, most probably because the company was so busy with its work on the Merlin. The same fate befell the Pennine, which was closely related to the Exe— and the Crecy did not even get as far as a test flight. This is perhaps a pity, for it was the most unorthodox Rolls-Royce of them all – a highly supercharged sleeve-valve two-stroke which was conceived as the gas producer for a compound piston/turbine engine.

Nevertheless the Merlin was not the last important piston engine contributed to aviation by Rolls-Royce. Just after the outbreak of war they thought of an expanded Merlin to be called the Griffon: the capacity was increased by nearly 36 percent, making the Griffon equal in swept volume to the R, but by clever redesign they kept its overall length virtually the same as that of the Merlin, its frontal area insignificantly greater, and everything looked thoroughly promising until they dis-

RR did a lot of research into exhaust systems: for fighters they produced jet stacks which developed forward thrust and were reckoned more worthwhile than turbochargers, for intruders such as these Mosquito bombers they devised flame-quenchers and even silencers

Clever rearrangement of auxiliary drives allowed the 36-litre RR Griffon to occupy the same space as the 27-litre Merlin, as in this Spitfire

covered that it was much too heavy. The second version was prepared for test by June 1940 after some extremely hard work, but the engine did not go into production until March 1942. It was originally asked for by the Admiralty, who wanted a really powerful engine suitable for torpedo bombers and other low-altitude ship-borne aircraft. The Griffon filled the bill very well once it was put into production and it gradually got more and more powerful until eventually with two-stage three-speed supercharging it could maintain 2,000 horsepower up to 20,000 feet. Many of the later Spitfires were powered by it, as well as the Fleet Air Arm machines for which it was originally devised, and it saw service for many years

after the war in Lincoln and Shackleton aircraft operating under the aegis of Coastal Command, carrying out long-range maritime reconnaissance operations.

By this time the Rolls-Royce aero engine effort was being diverted to gas turbines, as will be told in a later chapter, but they had one more big banger to reveal. This they had again chosen to call the Eagle, but it was like no other Eagle. In fact it was a clear copy of the Napier Sabre, a flat H sleeve-valve twenty-four cylinder engine which, developing 3,400hp, was roughly as powerful as a Sabre in service trim. Unfortunately for the comparison, it was much bigger at 46 litres, was clumsy in its dimensions and excessively heavy, weighing 3,900 lb. Furthermore it was abysmally unreliable and was hurriedly abandoned after a number of abortive test flights in the Westland Wyvern strike fighter. Despite all this, the propaganda

machine declared that the Eagle had been designed to show what an engine like the Napier Sabre could do if only it were made properly!

This bit of appalling cheek was the last of the many insults that had been heaped upon Napier by Rolls-Royce in their long-drawn-out feud. Right from the earliest days of motoring, Rolls-Royce seemed to have a morbid fear of competition from Napier. The disgraceful means by which they snatched Bentley away from Napier in 1931 added injury to insult, and left the two parties bitterly inimical for the next twenty years.

The way things were going, Rolls-Royce could afford to let Napier be indulged a little. They had waxed and grown fat as the war went on, and only occasionally did they copy Jeshurun and kick. Their factory expansion was quite fantastic during the period of war effort. 'It is fitting,' said a publicity handout with typical smugness, 'in the time of extreme crisis through which we have now happily passed, for the country to expect from Rolls-Royce a supreme achievement'). This supreme achievement could be measured as well on the ground as in the air. In 1935 the Derby factory covered 803,000 square feet, and 7,835 people worked there. By 1939 the factory had been greatly expanded and additional premises added at Crewe so that the floor area was now twice as great as in 1935 while the personnel strength rose to 12,500. By 1941 dispersal and evacuation premises had been allotted to Derby and to Crewe – which had itself grown more than somewhat – and vast new factory accommodation had been taken over in Glasgow: the shop area was now six times that of 1935. In 1943 it was 8.2 times as great; and in 1944, with a total of 7,228,520 square feet, the shop area was nine times as great, housing a total of 57,067 personnel. We need not bother to ask whence the money came.

115

THE SKY IS THE LIMIT

The story of the gas turbine in Britain goes back a long way, even before 1930 when Whittle was granted his first patent. The difficulties and delays which impeded the development of these early ideas have all been recorded in print, and their recital would be out of place here; but the fact that there was some activity may be taken as background to the interest formed by Rolls-Royce in gas turbines some time about 1939. What got them interested is not known: most probably they had found out by some means that Bristol, one of their great rivals in the British Aviation industry, had done a lot of theoretical work on the subject in 1938. As it happens, Bristol had by the spring of 1942 completed the design of what was to become known after the war as the Theseus turboprop, a power plant whose specific fuel consumption was as good as that of many first class piston engines at a time when gas turbines were generally recognised as being excessively thirsty.

First British jet to go operational, twice breaker of the world speed record, the Gloster Meteor went through many variations but was famous in its early days with the still rather tentative RR turbines. It also acted as flying test bed for the first turboprop engines

It is unlikely that Rolls-Royce visualised this in 1939, though they might well have anticipated Bristol's decision to delay development of the gas turbine during the war because of pressure of work on piston engines. Be that as it may, Rolls-Royce were convinced that the engine of the distant and temporally unpredictable future would be the gas turbine, and in the absence of anybody on its staff who could undertake the necessary studies they took onto their staff A A Griffiths, who was at that time employed at the Royal Aircraft Establishment. He then resumed with Rolls-Royce his studies of a gas turbine which was originally intended to be used as ducted fan, although the basic unit was capable of being used as the basis of either a turbojet or turboprop just as well. From the middle of 1939, when Griffith came to Rolls-Royce, to the beginning of 1941 was spent in doing preliminary calculations and a limited amount of combustion testing, and very few men were involved. In the spring of 1941 however, Rolls-Royce suddenly gave the project a very high priority with the result that the engine was run on compressed air in October of that year. Not until 1943 could it run under its own power, for lack of a suitable combustion system of its own, but by then Rolls-Royce was engaged in a new line of business that had originally been earmarked by the government for exploitation by other companies.

The formation of Power Jets by the government as a more or less independent but subsidised company specialising in the development of the gas turbine was followed in the early stages of the Second World War by the farming out of similar work to Metropolitan Vickers, to De Havilland, and to Rover. Unfortunately, relations between Power Jets and Rover became very strained because the two firms failed to see eye to eye on many matters; and Rolls-Royce seem to have been able to take advantage of this ill-feeling. By the end of 1941 they had overcome the worst of their problems in development of the Merlin engine –

problems that had for at least two years constituted a real crisis not only in the history of the company but also, if we did but know it, in the history of the nation – and now they were able to devote a certain amount of time to the development of turbojets as well as working on Griffith's turboprop. Rolls-Royce were recognised as experts in supercharger design and development, with such great justification as we have remarked in an earlier chapter; and since the compressor of a gas turbine was an analogous mechanism it was only natural that the relevant expertise of Rolls-Royce should be employed where possible. Stanley Hooker of Rolls-Royce volunteered a certain amount of assistance which Rover and Power Jets seemed glad to accept, and by December 1941 Rolls-Royce had a foot firmly in the door, helping to build experimental compressors for the other two companies, and designing a new diffuser for the latest version of the Whittle engine (the W2B).

From this situation there emerged in January 1942 a sub-contract from Power Jets, awarded after discussions between Rolls-Royce and the Air Ministry had been expanded to include that company, which provided for Rolls-Royce to design and develop a turbojet of its own, to be known as the WR1. The idea was that it should be done in close collaboration with Power Jets, that it should provide a means whereby Rolls-Royce could gain experience with the new type of engine, and that Rolls-Royce were at liberty to depart from the design principles expounded by Whittle in any respect they chose. In fact they copied Whittle fairly faithfully, apart from relying on their own experience when it came to the aerodynamic design of the compressor, and two engines were built and tested before the end of 1942. By this time the W2B was coming along well and the Rolls-Royce engine was abandoned as already out of date. In its place was to go the W2B, the direct responsibility

for which was handed to Rolls-Royce on a plate by Rover with the full approval of the government. Rolls-Royce only transferred a dozen or so of their development engineers to turbine work, but about the same number came to them from Rover. All work on other Rolls-Royce turbine projects was stopped forthwith, saving only the Griffith engine which persisted until late 1944.

Although this had been going on in 1942, formal responsibility was not assumed by Rolls-Royce until 1st April 1943. By that time they had done a lot of work on the existing Whittle-type turbine by standardising on the use of Nimonic nickel-alloy turbine blades machined to size (there had been a great deal of intensive metallurgical work done on turbine blade materials both by the British and the Americans in the immediately preceding years, and by the Germans too) and then intensely developing the techniques of production. Before Rolls-Royce took over formally, Rover had put the

What really put turboprops on the map was the phenomenally successful Vickers Viscount, powered by four RR Dart engines which were in their day equally remarkable

machine through a twenty-five-hour test at the design rating of 1,500 lb static thrust; and as soon as it was theirs, Rolls-Royce took the Welland (as the engine then became known) through a full 100-hour type test at the same rating. Two months later the Welland flew – a pair of them, indeed, in a Gloster Meteor, cleared for 1,400 lb thrust per engine in the first flight and 1,600 lb thereafter. It was soon found that the engine surged at high altitudes, and a lot of subsequent work was done on this problem without a complete solution ever being found.

The Welland was put into production in October 1943 and the first production examples were delivered, in May the following year. Powered by a brace of these, the Mark I Gloster Meteor

RR met stiffer competition in gas
turbines than in anything else they
ever tried, but were not without
their successes – such as the Avon
turbojet, which served in many
famous military and civil aircraft,
including the Hawker Siddeley
Comet. In the days when the Comet
was made by de Havilland, then of
course it had de Havilland turbojets

could reach a speed of about 410mph at sea level, barely enough to qualify it for duty intercepting the flying bombs that the Germans began to direct towards England in August 1944. At about this time, let us remember, the Messerschmitt Me 262 twin-jet fighter was going into service with a speed of 520mph at sea level.

Some time before this, Rolls-Royce had plans for a different approach to gas turbine design, based on plans formulated by Rover who had argued back in 1941 that the reverse-flow combustion system of the Whittle engine was inferior to the straight-through type that they felt should be investigated. When Rolls-Royce took over Rover's work in 1943 they reached the same conclusion, and they developed the prototype straight-through Rover engine to produce what became known as the Rolls-Royce Derwent 1. This was first tested in July 1943, did a 100-hour type test at 2,000 lb thrust in November, and flew in the following March. By November 1944 it was in production, and it made the Meteor a good 50mph faster than before.

It was not long before Rolls-Royce felt confident that they could design their own engines completely from scratch without having to be hampered by limitations of existing designs. The first such engine was to be the Nene, and Government assigned it the highest possible priority in 1944, perturbed as they were by the impressive rate of development of the turbojet in Germany. With this ministerial encouragement Rolls-Royce had the Nene running in October 1944, and before much longer it was running well, giving 4,500 lb thrust.

Unfortunately there were no aircraft around to make practical use of it. So in January 1945 it was decided that plans for the production of the Derwent 4 (the latest version of the original Rover Whittle design) should be abandoned and a scaled-down version of the Nene substituted. This lesser Nene went into production straight off the drawing board, an astonishing demonstration of faith at that stage of the game, and it was christened the Derwent 5. Its service rating was 3,500 lb thrust for 1,260 lb weight, and its specific fuel consumption would have looked good at 1 lb per lb thrust per hour were it not for that blessed Bristol we mentioned earlier. Two special Derwent 5s were then uprated to 4,000 lb each, put in a Meteor 4 that was completely standard except for the removal of its armaments, and set a new world speed record of 606mph in November 1945. This was the first British jet-propelled fighter to equal, let alone surpass so generously, the performance of the German Me 262, so it was quite a good way to start the peace. In the following year the Meteor pushed the record up to 616mph, but Whittle's work was now no more than a memory. The same applied to Rover; and as for Power Jets, they had suffered the ultimate ignominy of being nationalised in April 1944.

Twenty-seven years later, as this is being written, we are waiting for Rolls-Royce to be nationalised in their turn – not, as in the case of Power Jets, so that the government could direct the sort of work they should do, but because they were in such dire financial straits that no other course seemed open. They had been doing so well, too. In September 1945 the first turboprop had flown, a Gloster Meteor with experimental Rolls-Royce engine. In July 1948 the first turboprop airliner, the Vickers Viscount, flew, powered by four Rolls-Royce Darts; and twelve months later the De Havilland Comet became the world's first turbojet air liner to fly, soon to revolutionise civil aviation with the aid of four Rolls-Royce Avon gas turbines. By 1963 the latest version of the Dart set a new record in aero

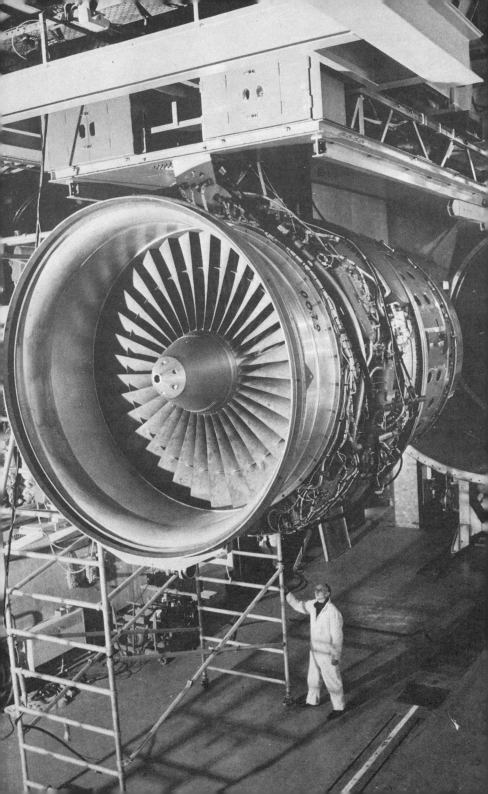

engine reliability, becoming the first in the world to be approved to run for 4,000 hours without requiring overhaul. This impressive Rolls-Royce achievement meant in effect that these engines could be flown for about 800,000 miles without having to be taken out of service : so the Viscounts which shuttled about on short and medium-haul journeys all over the world could achieve prodigies of utilisation. Likewise the Avon jet engine had gradually had its overhaul life extended to 3,000 hours, equivalent to a million miles between overhauls, and three times the working life of this engine when the Comets went into service in 1960. In even less time the Rolls-Royce Tyne turboprop which powered the Vanguard liner had its overhaul life extended from 400 to 1,250 hours.

In almost every branch of aviation, Rolls-Royce enjoyed a marvelous reputation. For light aircraft there were the air-cooled Continental horizontally-opposed piston engines which Rolls-Royce were licenced to build and maintain on behalf of the American company. Air-liners, maritime reconnaissance planes, fighters, bombers everything in the air was a likely user of Rolls-Royce power plants. The company had come a long way from the difficult years after the World War when they had unconvincingly spent a fortune in trying to give the Merlin sufficient reliability for it to be economically viable for commercial aviation. In the 1960s Rolls-Royce could boast that every minute of the day and night, somewhere in the world, a Rolls-Royce-powered aircraft would be taking off.

Of course they had competition. The Americans were now making some superb aero engines of their own that did not owe anything to British inspiration. The Russians had some gas turbines whose thrust was quite prodigious. And in Britain there were still the arch-enemies Bristol, as well as Armstrong Siddeley and De Havilland, turning out aero engines that were frequently as good as Rolls-Royce could produce and sometimes appreciably better.

During the course of these developments the British Government had formed the inflexible view that the days when various private enterprises should compete with one another for the limited amount of work that the aviation business could give them had passed. There should be only one or at the most two manufacturers of aircraft, only one maker of aero engines. Accordingly the Government set about reorganising the aviation industry of Britain : little by little, companies were encouraged or forced to amalgamate ; then the composite firms thus created would be joined together, and finally the whole lot would merge into one single organisation. By 1968 the process was virtually complete and it was Rolls-Royce which had acquired all the others. The source that once gave us De Havilland engines of almost every sort from small light fours to supersonic jets became part of the Rolls-Royce Small Engines Division. The almighty Bristol Olympus became the Rolls-Olympus, and so on all down the line.

A nearby offshoot of the Bristol parent firm at Filton was among the companies taken into the growing Rolls-Royce organisation, and Bristol Aeroplane Plastics Limited became Rolls-Royce Composite Materials. They also became crucially important, for Rolls-Royce had been working hard on the development of carbon fibres as a reinforcement material for plastics, one that would produce a composite material of unrivalled strength: weight ratio. The Americans had been pursuing the same enquiries with regard to boron, but boron fibres were much more difficult to manage and very much more expensive. In 1970 the successful near-culmination of Rolls-Royce's work was being ballyhooed

Intended to power the huge Lockheed Tri-Star airbus, the RB211 was enormous, looking even more so in the test house

May 1971: Mr I T Morrow, the new deputy chairman and managing director of the new Rolls-Royce (1971) Ltd, signs with the chairman of Lockheed Aircraft Corporation (centre) a conditional contract covering the supply of RB211 engines for Tri-Star airlines. Lockheed's lawyer looks happy with the arrangements

in every conceivable medium, with particular emphasis being laid on the fact that the new material was playing a vital part in the design and development of the Rolls-Royce RB211 turbofan jet engine. An 'advanced technology turbofan engine', Rolls-Royce called the RB211. It was one of a whole new generation of them that were being developed furiously and expensively during the latter half of the 1960s. Turbofans had been the great preoccupation of the aero engine division for years – and with the aero engine division now the greatest part of the organisation, turbofans were therefore an undertaking of no mean order. What with the industrial and marine turbines, the little piston engines, and the wide range of turbofans, turbojets, turboprops, turboshafts, ramjets and rocket engines, the division accounted for most of the 20,000 or so on the payroll whose duties were in research, design and development – a quarter of the company's total strength.

The first great turbofan was the two-spool Conway, used in versions of the Boeing 707 and Douglas DC8 transports, as well as being standard in the VC 10, the Super VC 10, and the Handley Page Victor B Mk 2. In 1959 design of the Spey began, and this led to civil versions for the Hawker Siddeley Trident, the BAC 111 and the Grumman Gulfstream, while the military Spey not only powered the Hawker Siddeley Buccaneer but also significantly supplanted America's own General Electric 879 turbojet in the McDonnel Phantom, amongst others. These two-spool turbofans were eminently successful, and did the company

and the country a lot of good, morally and materially. The three-spool types promised to do even better, and in 1966 the first of them, the Trent, was announced. This ushered in the 'advanced technology' of which the company was so proud. The idea of this new family of engines was that they should achieve a specific fuel consumption 25 per cent lower than engines currently in service, be quiet (especially on approach) and light, and yet feature reliability and a long overhaul life.

The low noise level resulted from the use of a single-stage independent controllable-speed fan without intake guide vanes. The low specific fuel consumption was engineered by high compression ratio and high by-pass ratio. The other qualities resulted mainly from simple mechanical construction with no variable stators or compressor bleed valves, and it all looked tremendously promising. With 180 airlines and sixty air forces on their books, Rolls-Royce had plenty of customers to keep happy; and in the

late 1960s it seemed that the 45,000
aero-engines that carried the company's banner around the world might
be the prelude to even greater things.
Next after the Trent were to be the RB
207 for the European Airbus, and con-
currently the RB 211. The publicists
loved the 211: we saw it installed for
flight testing in the tail of a VC 10 at the
SBAC Farnborough air display, hustling
the big airliner unaided across the
arena at low altitude in a silence broken
only by the excited praise of the public-
address commentary. 'Marvellous performance,' they assured us, 'and a
tremendous commercial future' – not
only for the engine, but also for the
new Rolls-Royce wonder material of
which the intake fan was composed.

The huge 'blades of the fan were
being made of carbon fibre reinforced
plastics, endowing the power unit with
a combination of performance and
economy that could not be rivalled by
anything else in production or under
development. No less a company than
Lockheed of America negotiated to use

it as the power unit of their new Tri-
Star Transport aircraft, and this, it was
thought, could only mean lots more
valuable export business for Britain.

But as 1970 wore on it began to be
apparent that the contract price was too
low, that the contractual delivery dates
were too early, and that the contractual
penalty clauses were too harsh. Rolls-
Royce had misjudged the difficulties
that stood in their way, and misjudged
their ability to cope with them. They
had also made a critical error in the
carbon fibre parts for the RB 211: the
engine might work well in a test rig,
but when tried in flight it could not deal
with the occasional passing bird that
every airborne jet engine must be able
to ingest: the fan blades simply
shattered.

What, in these circumstances, could
Rolls-Royce do? They might look for a
new miracle material, beg for time,
cadge for money, pray for mercy, or
go bankrupt. At the time of writing it
seems likely that they will complete the
course and do all five.

WAIT TILL THE CLOUDS ROLL BY

The Britain that emerged from the war in 1945 was victorious but exhausted. The exhaustion was not only material and physical but also moral and spiritual; and when the immediate post-war years proved to impose upon the nation an austerity which was in many respects more severe than had been suffered during the war, it was with a mixture of resignation and resentment that the people turned to the task of putting the country back on its feet. The *status quo ante bellum* was beyond restoration – and in any case the younger half of the population, appalled by the war and judging it to be the consequence of an ill-regulated mode of life and an enervated establish-

The Phantom 4 was a limited-series straight-8 for very special customers. Mulliner produced this one to the special order of HRH Princess Margaret

ment in the years preceding it, had no wish to return to that state of affairs. It was a new world that they wanted, fair rather than brave. As for the older half of the population, dispirited and dispossessed, they were generally just too tired to try to regain what had seemed to many of them an all too careless rapture.

In this far from favourable climate, how should Rolls-Royce resume their business of making and selling cars? Taxation, petrol rationing and material shortages of every kind made it clear that this was no place for such gargantuan extravagances as the Phantom 3; but if it was clear that such a car was not wanted, it was much more difficult to establish clearly what was wanted. Rolls-Royce could draw upon their experience in the years following the end of the Great War in 1918, but the most valuable lesson to be derived from that experience was merely that they should not make the same mistake again. In 1919 Rolls-Royce had dropped the aero engine business, striving instead to provide Silver Ghosts for all those fortunate people who had survived the war with plenty of money – many of them with far more than they had possessed when it started. After two years the bubble had burst and it was a chastened Rolls-Royce that had to beg for favours from the Air Ministry. In 1945 things were very different: on the one hand, conspicuous consumption was shunned by all but the most insensitive (though everyone was anxious to go motoring again); on the other hand, recent developments with the gas turbine had shown Rolls-Royce that they had whole new worlds to conquer in aviation, and the already imminent Cold War could keep them profitably engaged in the armaments race. Nevertheless it was expected of Rolls-Royce that they should start making cars again and they themselves were anxious to do so, re-organising their factory accommodation at Crewe for the purpose.

Some sort of compromise was called for in design. Behemoths were out of

the question; but a small Rolls-Royce, however practical, would not be a real Rolls-Royce. Standards of quality, finish, quietness, smoothness and performance had to be maintained at what was generally recognised as Rolls-Royce level; but the car had to be of moderate size. In the pre-war Wraith and Bentley Mark 5 the car division, now under Dr Llewellyn-Smith (Lord Hives was now chairman) sought and found their inspiration.

Some things would have to be changed. Perhaps most important, cars that were to be sold overseas had to be bodied somewhat differently, for traditional coachbuilding techniques and materials did not produce results that were suitable in climates and environments more extreme and aggressive than those of Britain and Europe. Already in the late pre-war years Rolls-Royce had taken a step towards standardisation of bodies by assimilating Park Ward, whose standard steel bodies (especially on the Mark 5) had shown that traditional British styling could be agreeably updated and adapted to line production. For their postwar cars Rolls-Royce went a step further and produced a design for the new Bentley, the Mark 6, that would be stamped out in quantities by the Pressed Steel Company along with all the refrigerators and Morris Tens and the like – though hopefully to somewhat higher standards. On the whole their hopes were fulfilled, but the poor quality of available materials was something that could not be circumvented even with Rolls-Royce influence. The consequences of this shortcoming could not be foreseen at the time but are all too evident today, when many a Mark 6 Bentley (and indeed some the the later S series) which started off as a couple of tons of motor car have become transformed into one and a half tons of car and half a ton of rust.

The engine also had to be changed. Scope for further development of the pre-war six-cylinder specimen was now limited by the impossibility of enlarging the valves and ports any

more; but the B series engine, already tried in some wartime experimental cars, seemed a promising substitute. With it Rolls-Royce reverted to the overhead inlet and side exhaust valve layout with which Royce had toyed in 1903. The 4-litre Bentley, which was the last car produced by W O before his company was taken over by Rolls-Royce, also had an F head of this type. When Rolls-Royce embarked on the design of the B series in 1938 they may have been influenced by these antecedents; they were certainly attracted by the possibility of making a notably quiet engine with ample valve sizes and the minimum of valve operating mechanism.

As developed for military purposes the B engine was made in four-, six-, and eight-cylinder versions, with iron blocks or with aluminium; but for car production the simple iron six was adopted almost as a foregone conclusion. It was not a bad engine; indeed in some respects Rolls-Royce had done quite well in its development. For example they reached a satisfactory conclusion to their long search for a crankshaft that would not too severely handicap the engine's performance: with a simple and somewhat improbable looking arrangement

On a Silver Wraith chassis for 'hoi-polloi' Mulliner's 7-passenger limousine looked like the Royal Phantom

of balance weights and with more and more attention to balancing (eventually they even got around to installing a dynamic balancer, something that had long been used as a matter of course by their more respectable rivals) this big six could spin safely up to 5,400 rev/min. It was an engine that was betrayed by some of its details, however; early bypass oil filter systems simply were not good enough and many a bearing was ruined by dirt. The chromium plated cylinder bores (just the upper half of the bore was plated) gave good service in some cases but in many others the chrome was quickly worn away and thereafter attrition of the liner material was very rapid indeed. The solution to this problem was to eliminate the chrome plating and insert a short half-liner with a 30 percent chrome content. Even so, bore lubrication and piston seizure became troublesome and it took two years for a new shape of piston to complete a list of modifications that more or less cured the problem.

It was an engine endowed with many

Above : The Park Ward touring limousine made the Silver Wraith look much more plebeian
Below : Looking like a mark 6 Bentley with a RR radiator, the Silver Dawn was the first attempt to standardise a steel body for export

mixed blessings. The electrical system, for example, was typical of Rolls-Royce's growing tendencies to farm out work to specialists rather than try to do everything themselves. Where once Royce's own superb electrical equipment had distinguished the cars that bore his name, now there was an assortment of components supplied by Lucas albeit specially prepared by the exhibition department at CAV, and in some cases specially designed or modified to meet a Rolls-Royce specification.

The distributor was a Delco-Remy twin-point device well known for giving accurate timing at high speeds: and if a driver was caught by a points failure, he only had to swallow his pride and go to the nearest Bedford truck spares depot in order to get replacement points. Provided he had the necessary special tools he could synchronize the points in not much more than half a day.

In many such respects the post-war Bentley, and the Rolls-Royce chassis which was essentially similar, were much more humdrum than their pre-war counterparts. The changes were not made without a good deal of experiment and enquiry at Crewe, but the new did not necessarily have to perform better than the old: it would suffice if it were as good, or practically as good, and cheaper. Thus the riveting and bolting of the chassis was extensively replaced by welding; the centre-lock wheels were replaced by crude multiple-stud affairs trimmed by gay deceiver nave plates; the water pump and dynamo were now driven by belt instead of by gears; and whereas once everything was inspected and each new car was road tested over about 350 miles, now inspection was on a batch basis and 150 miles testing was deemed sufficient.

Such then was the Mark 6 Bentley which went into production in 1946, a brave effort in a drab new world, a nice car and a good car, but by no means faultless. Because it was a Bentley it had two carburettors and well spaced ratios in the gearbox, but this did not stop Rolls-Royce from pursuing their eternal search for high torque at low revs, and a heavy flywheel and mild valve timing made it possible to drive the car slowly – as most people did. The compression ratio was low, only 6.4:1, partly due to the fact that the 'pool' petrol, the only fuel available to private motorists at the time, was perfectly foul stuff of low octane rating and partly because the awkward shape of the combustion chamber so corrupted flame travel that the engine simply refused to take a higher compression ratio even when better fuels were tried. For all its ability to pull well at low speeds, it was not as smooth as Rolls-Royce engines had previously been. However, the occupants of the car were well insulated from it, and provided they were not being driven in too sporting a manner they could look down from their thrones with all the positive satisfaction of those who have 'made it' and could muse indulgently on the lower orders who had not. When driven hard the Bentley was a little less reassuring, for the steering felt sloppy and roll in corners took the front wheels to some rather unfavourable angles. But by the standards of its time, the car had a good straight-line performance and this was all that mattered to most customers, if indeed they were concerned with performance at all. More commonly the car was bought unhesitatingly, unthinkingly and uncritically, without examination of its shortcomings or consideration of whether there might not be something better available.

This was even more true of the Rolls-Royce equivalent, the Silver Wraith, which went into production as a chassis in 1947 for clothing with bodywork by the remaining specialist coachbuilders. In its Rolls-Royce form the engine had but one carburettor and an even milder camshaft, and when this impediment was combined with the burden of an extra heavy body on the long wheelbase version, the performance of the Silver Wraith was very leisurely indeed. It was still a pleasant car in which to

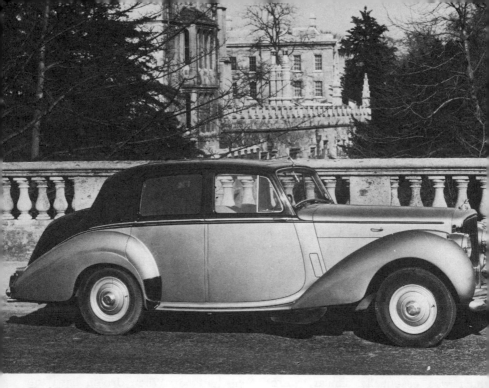

As for the mark 6 Bentley, it was obviously derived from the mark 5 and the Corniche. Growing a bigger luggage boot and then a bigger engine, it finished as the R-type Bentley

make a long journey on easy roads; it was still a quiet car, a refined car, a comfortable and sometimes even an elegant car; but it was hardly an exportable car, so in 1949 the Silver Dawn was added to the catalogue, virtually a Rolls-Royce version of the standard steel Mark 6 Bentley, initially for export only but eventually put on to the home market as well.

These two Rolls-Royce machines stayed in the catalogues for several years, the Silver Dawn until 1955 and the Silver Wraith until 1959. They did not endure without suffering some changes, such as were to summon more attention when they were visited on the Bentley. The first of these was an increase in cylinder bore from $3\frac{1}{2}$ to $3\frac{5}{8}$ inches in 1951. This step, which

increased the capacity from 4,257 cm to 4,566 cm^3, was taken in response to demands for more performance: it was the only alternative to raising the compression ratio (which the engine would not stand) and it was a very effective improvement. With this engine the car was known as 'the big bore Bentley' and some would say that the phrase's ambiguity was probably justified.

The following year the big bore was supplemented by a big boot and by an optional automatic transmission, and the Mark 6 became the R type Bentley for which there is little to be said except that from it was developed another model of considerable merit and outstanding beauty, the R-type Continental. With its engine even further bored out to a capacity of nearly 4.9 litres, with a gearbox of beautifully close ratios and with a streamlined aluminium panelled body of imposing elegance and fair efficiency, this car appeared as a prototype in all sorts of improbable locations, and was even to be seen acting as a mobile stewards' enclosure n the Le Mans circuit during the 24-our sports car race, where it actually assed some of the smaller competitors n the straights. Indeed it would do early 120mph, and could just exceed 00 in third gear. It was a beautiful ar and a fast car, the sort of car that entleys were supposed to be. It andled reasonably well in the dry, 10ugh it wore its tyres out at a pheno-1enal rate if driven hard, but in the wet was best driven very gently.

During the run of the R-type, which nished in 1955, 207 Continentals were 1ade, all but sixteen of them with that 1perb swept-tail body by H J Mulliner.

 looked enormous, though in width, 1ngth and height it was actually the 1me as the R-type. What made it erform so well, apart from the better 1ape, was its better power: weight 1tio, deriving not only from the bigger 1gine but also from lighter construc-on; the car weighed over 500 lb less 1an the standard R-type.

Seeing the obvious success of the 1larged engine, Bentley and Rolls-oyce enthusiasts began to speculate 1riously about what the factory's 1ext move might be. Since 1950 a few 1ecial Rolls-Royce limousines had 1een constructed for Royalty and Heads f State only, the huge cars (wheelbase 1as 145 inches, the rear track 63) 1eing powered by the straight-8 ver-1on of the B engine such as had 1owered Big Bertha during the war and 1as still being developed for military 1pplications. Rolls-Royce had said quite 1rmly that this car, the Phantom 4, was 1 be a very limited edition, but that 1as the sort of motor industry dis-1aimer that people had learned not to 1elieve implicitly. What about the 1.9-litre six for the 'standard' cars, 1entley and Rolls-Royce alike, and then 1 straight 8 for a new Continental?

That such ideas could be entertained 1as certainly a sign of the times. 1ore performance was being deman-1ed, the age of austerity was giving 1ay to the age of easy credit, and 1onspicuous consumption was begin-1ing to be fashionable. Automobile

Lord Hives (first baron, created 1950) who started with the company as E W Hives in the early days of the Silver Ghost and eventually became its chairman

engineering had made enormous strides, and already there were cars with petrol injection, with disc brakes, with self-levelling suspension, and with body contours aerodynamically refined in wind tunnels. With all the special knowledge gleaned from their engineering for the aviation industry, what might not Rolls-Royce do next?

What they did was bitterly disap-pointing. In 1955, under the guise of the Silver Cloud (as a Rolls-Royce) they produced a car driven by the 4.9-litre six-cylinder engine with a low com-pression ratio, installed with automatic transmission in a body which was big and ugly, a car that was heavy, ill-handling and a prey to rust.

Apart from the radiators there was no difference between the S type and the Silver Cloud. The propaganda machine dealt with this piece of flagrant badge engineering by saying that of course no new Rolls-Royce could be regarded as quite satisfactory unless it were just as fast as a Bentley, while a Bentley owner was entitled to expect just as much quietness and refinement in his car as he might find in a Rolls-Royce.

The Silver Cloud began life with a 6-cylinder 4.9-litre engine related to that of . . .

Applied to the hardware, this philosophy led in the following year to the appearance of the S-type Continental, a car with nothing like the grace of the R-type Continental nor its point-to-point pace – for that beautiful close-ratio synchromesh gearbox had been supplanted by the standard automatic. If you were insistent and were prepared to wait, you could buy an S-type Continental with synchromesh gearbox, but few people did: by 1956, anybody who wanted a genuine Grand Touring car and planned to enjoy driving it was taking his custom elsewhere. People who bought Bentleys were mainly the sort of people who liked to be seen as the sort of people who bought Bentleys.

Now there is nothing wrong with the idea of automatic transmission; I am all in favour of it, and do not think that a car can be considered truly modern without it. The trouble with the S-type

was that it was not a modern car and the automatic transmission was not a good one. It was not Rolls-Royce's own, of course, but was bought from General Motors, who were by now established as one of the principal sources of technical inspiration for the Rolls-Royce car division. By the time Rolls-Royce had finished developing it, refining it and improving it, bottom and second gear were so low as to be virtually indistinguishable, the third gear ran out at about 65mph, and the quite lively acceleration up to 60 that had been provided by these low ratios suddenly deteriorated and the car eventually ran into its limiting headwind at about 105mph. Considering the bulk of the car and its considerable weight (two tons at the kerb) this was a tolerable performance, but it you drove it like that for long you would be lucky to achieve twelve miles per gallon, in which case the limited range permitted by the eighteen-gallon tank once again inhibited its use on long journeys. seems a pity that the manufacturers di not (except to special order, which was rare) provide a petrol tank of a size to match the scale and appetite of the car.

The appetites of the customers were growing even more insatiable. They still wanted their cars big, and the Silver Wraith had to be even more spacious and sumptuous than the Silver Cloud. The customer also demanded adequate performance in the traffic-lights sprint, but this heavyweight could not hope to acquit itself well while powered by the old over-extended 6-cylinder engine. Something considerably more than its 178bhp would be required, if possible without making the car any longer than it was already. Accordingly, as in the Phantom 3 which succeeded the six-in-line Phantom 2, a V engine would be necessary.

But not a V12. It would have been out of keeping with the character of the car, whereas it was appropriate that the new engine should be a V8. All manner of big easy-going American cars had demonstrated that a simple V8 with overhead valves could provide plenty of low-speed power and reasonable high-speed smoothness, provided that it were made big enough and the porting were made sufficiently constricting. And after all, since the rest of the car had so much in common with American practice (body styling only excepted), what could be more natural than to incorporate a power unit such as the American market might understand ?

In one respect Rolls-Royce failed to achieve the American ideal. The foundry techniques that permitted the major American manufacturers to produce iron engine castings of low weight (due to very thin walls) were beyond British abilities, so the Rolls-Royce V8 was cast

. . . the R–type Bentley Continental, a worthy heir to the tradition of the Continental Phantom 2 and the mark 5 Bentley Corniche

Cloud 3 encounters the night-life of
Monté Carlo

But the advent of the V8 Silver Cloud 2 forced the end of the R-type Continental Bentley, and the S-type Continental was (in Park Ward drophead form) frankly uninspiring ...

in aluminium alloy. Perhaps because of this and despite the self-adjusting hydraulic tappets, the new V8 was noisier than a representative American engine of similar size, weight and power output. In fact the size was 6.23-litres, and on a compression ratio of 8:1 the engine could produce an easy 230bhp.

Now the car enjoyed extremely good performance. By the standards of 1959 when the S2/Silver Cloud 2 was introduced with the new engine, its acceleration was quite dramatic: from a standstill it could reach 60mph in ten seconds, 100 in about 35 (the S1 took 50) and could reach about 117mph. The wide-ratio automatic transmission still made its contribution to the vivid step-off and left the driver at the mercy of top gear from 72mph upwards; but it was a much livelier top gear than before. Indeed even the Phantom 5, with the same engine in an outsize chassis for the carriage-building trade, could sprint quite effectively beneath the burden of a huge limousine body, and comfortably exceed 100mph.

For most purposes the S2 was quite nippy enough, its kerb weight having risen to nearly 4,600lb. This made mandatory the power-assisted steering that had been introduced as an option a little earlier on the 6-cylinder car, but the solution was not entirely satisfactory. The lightness that had been sought had been found, and the mechanism and linkages were satisfactorily robust; but the steering had little feel and was extremely low-geared, no advantage having been taken of the servo to raise the steering ratio to provide quicker and more accurate response. Rolls-Royce defended the new steering by invoking what they

... or (as a Mulliner sports saloon) downright inept

called the 'sneeze factor', arguing that high-geared steering was dangerous since a quick movement of the wheel at high speeds might lead to the car actually going where it was directed.

What worried most people far more than the steering was the company's stubborn retention of drum brakes at a time when all other respectable cars had adopted discs. The publicity department countered such objections with the assurance that when Rolls-Royce found a disc brake that was as safe, as powerful, as consistent, and as quiet as their drum brake they would use it. Furthermore it could not be too widely known that Rolls-Royce brakes were subjected to protracted testing, in the course of which they were called upon repeatedly to stop the car from 70mph at intervals of one minute. Rolls-Royce brakes, said the propaganda, do not fade.

Recalling the lively acceleration of the V8, it can be seen that in stopping the car from 70mph once a minute the brakes need never bring it to a halt in less than 40 seconds. This involves

142

The Silver Cloud 3 drophead shared several body parts with the standard four-door saloon

retardation at a mere 0.253g, which is not the sort of deceleration that should induce fade.

In fact of course the brakes could reveal a considerably better performance than this, being designed in the unconventional but quite effective Rolls-Royce style as big drums with trailing shoes whose anti-fade negative-servo behaviour was compensated by a traditional Hispano-inspired Rolls-Royce mechanical servo. It is quite true that Rolls-Royce drum brakes do not fade – but the friction-driven servo does! From personal experience I can testify that the prospect of a roundabout approaching 2½ tons of brakeless S-type at three-figure speeds is not made any more attractive by the knowledge that the brakes could really be made to work if only the servo would provide

some effective means of communication with them. I have encountered the same servo fade in a Mark 6 Bentley, which suggests to me that by 1959 the company should have been aware of the hazard.

Perhaps the company's most urgent enquiries were into marketing requirements, for, in 1962, a third version of the Cloud appeared, mechanically similar to the second but with a raised compression ratio, improved interior heating and ventilation, and quadruple headlamps which in my view made the car uglier than ever.

In retrospect the S3 appears to have been a stopgap, facelifted to keep things going while the company readied

Commonality of parts was firmly established by 1963, when the Silver Cloud 3 Rolls-Royce and the S3 Bentley had to be compared closely to ensure that the Bentley was as quiet as the RR . . .

. . . and the RR as fast as the Bentley

a new design that had been on its way for years, a car which, apart from the engine and transmission, was completely new. This was the Silver Shadow (the T series, in Bentley parlance), and when it was announced in 1965 it created something of a furore. All sorts of snap judgements were delivered on it, many of them critical and most of them ill-informed; and this was hardly surprising, for the Silver Shadow was perhaps the first modern Rolls-Royce since the 20hp Tourist Trophy model. Now that the dust has settled we can see that Rolls-Royce deserve to be congratulated on the Shadow, not so much for what they achieved as for what they set out to do.

To move its 2-ton bulk, the Silver Cloud had a 6.23-litre engine. This specimen is the SC2 of 1960; the SC3 had a higher compression ratio. Power, according to RR, was 'enough'. 'Barely' enough?

The Cloud had been an unsatisfactory car, combining much that was bad in contemporary practice with some of the worst of the traditional school. The quantities now being handled by Rolls-Royce were such as to make the old idea of a separate chassis and body burdensome, while many of the traditional features of the chassis conspired to give it an unsatisfactory ride, poor roadholding, indifferent handling, and a forbidding unwieldiness in modern traffic. In almost every respect the Shadow was an improvement—not just an improvement in the usual Rolls-Royce sense of a developed version, but something that to them must have seemed quite revolutionary.

The chassis had gone. The new car was of unitary construction, welded up from steel pressings in such a way as to have ample beam and torsional stiffness and to allow suspension loads to be fed in at a number of widely separated points in order to improve stress

distribution. It was therefore feasible to endow the car with independent suspension not only at the front but also at the rear, and this was done with praiseworthy thoroughness because the rear suspension was supplemented by a self-levelling control powered by a high-pressure hydraulic system manufactured under licence from Citroën.. With such a system available it was natural that the old mechanical brake servo should be dispensed with, while at the same time the drums were replaced by a fail-safe disc system.

The result was a car of exceptional interest and considerable merit. It was not perfect: early examples had rear springing of too low a rate and too little roll stiffness. There was also some criticism of the looks of the car, for the modern boxy styling was essentially self-effacing, the car no longer declaring itself unmistakably from all angles to be a Rolls-Royce. On the other hand the traditional Palladian radiator fitted more harmoniously into the front of the car than into anything that the

The Silver Cloud chassis was heavy, but very well stiffened. Note the elaborate central cross-bracing

company had built in the preceding thirty years. Of course it was only a dummy show, as it had been for at least a decade; but no Rolls-Royce would be the same without it, and in this latest manifestation it was low and wide, reverting gratefully to the proportions in which it began life under Royce's pencil.

Before long the rear suspension was stiffened, and the big 8.45-15 bias-ply tyres backed by optional 205-15 radials. It was the first time that Rolls-Royce had ever designed a suspension suitable for tyres of this type, another pleasing proof of their more modern approach. Shortly afterward the GM automatic transmission with its four gears and simple Föttinger fluid coupling was replaced by the more modern and infinitely superior Chrysler Torque-flite with three speeds and a convertor coupling, an automatic transmission which had been around for years and had yet to be bettered by anything in production. This not only made the car much more pleasant to drive but also yielded a considerably better performance, knocking a second or so off the time to 60mph, for instance.

Quiet and refined as ever, the Shadow was a Rolls-Royce that could be driven zestfully if required. It had the adhesion to make such driving possible and the structural integrity to make it safe. In fact the structure was a rewarding thing to study: theoretically a simple monocoque shell of stressed steel skin, it went some way towards chassis theories by having well-insulated subframes mounted at each end from which to hang the suspension, running gear and power pack. In effect there were two halves to the chassis, tied together by the body – something that several other manufacturers had been doing for years but which was quite new for Rolls-Royce.

A monocoque car can never insulate its occupants in quite the same way as a well designed car with a separate chassis. In the latter case, no matter how much the chassis itself may flex, a cunningly mounted body will disguise the fact. A stressed body cannot transmit the very considerable loads to which it is subjected without giving rise to the occasional noise, shock or vibration which can be detected by the occupants; but Rolls-Royce mount their sub-frames so that just one or two degrees of freedom might be taken out at each point or pair of points, the damped mountings being then designed so as to do their several jobs as well as possible. The result can be considered the best of both worlds, strong and silent.

Equally thorough were the services to brakes, suspension and auxiliary systems. They looked very complex and were, but everything was there for a purpose and developed to be as trouble-free as airminded engineers could make them. The hydraulic system for the brakes would do credit to a modern aeroplane, with two power-

The engine of a Phantom was always unlike that of any other car, until the Phantom 5 took the standard Silver Cloud V8. Its main speciality was a 12-feet wheelbase

assisted independent circuits supplemented by one direct one, plus the mechanical hand-brake, making a total of four separate systematic failures necessary before the car might be left without brakes. Power hydraulics served the self-levelling suspension and the steering as well, though the steering was still dreadfully low geared. All the other jobs – the minor ones such as opening the windows, raising the radio aerial, or adjusting the seats – were done by electric motors. Even the automatic transmission selector was electric with an emergency manual override. Go and sit in the driver's

Change at Crewe: unitary construction replaced the old chassis for the Silver Shadow and its T-series Bentley equivalent

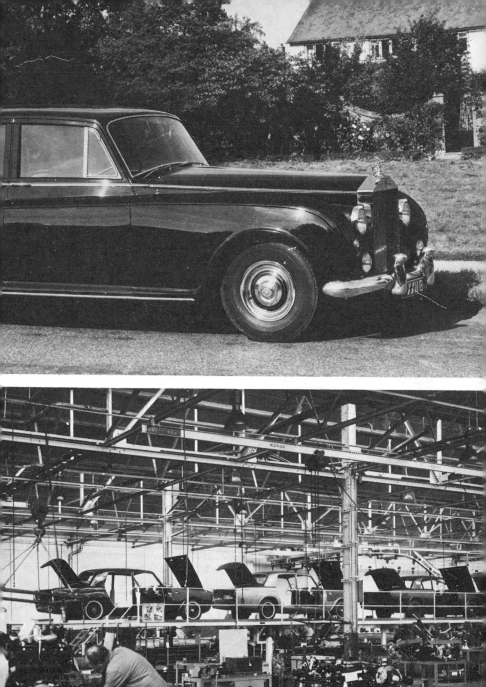

Line production and unitary construction notwithstanding, RR can still do a long long car for the limousine-minded. The long-wheelbase Shadow is more democratic than the old chauffeur-freezing de ville bodies, but the division is still there

seat and you can appreciate the good things in life, what Gray calls the 'pomp of power': twiddle a little joystick and the seat adjusts itself to chosen settings for leg room, seat height and rake, slowly and to the hum of electrics. Fine, firm comfortable seats they are too, and those in the rear are even better, giving the passengers plenty of lateral support. Behind them is a huge boot with a vast flat floor beneath which lurks the 24-gallon petrol tank that restores to this Rolls-Royce the ability to go for some serious motoring.

The handling of the Shadow is such as to make earnest high-speed driving on give-and-take roads a more realistic undertaking than in any previous Rolls-

Royce, but it is still a little intimidating. The very light and low-geared steering can be twirled without much misgiving, for the basic steering characteristic is strong understeer accompanied by considerable roll. Push the car to its cornering limit and it settles down to a steady widening of its line as the rear tyres cling tenaciously and the front ones drift outwards – though at the very ultimate extreme, the tail begins to come around and neutralise things. Never is there any feeling of impending sudden breakaway or control reversal; rather, it feels as though the car is looking after you and saving you from the consequences of anything rash that you might do. On fast open bends this is comforting, but in an unexpected tight corner greater immediacy of response would be more reassuring still.

One would not have thought from seeing them on the road that many Shadows were driven in this way. Nevertheless there must have been considerable customer demand for a faster and more controllable car, for

that is just what was made public in March 1971 as this book was being completed. It was called the Corniche, reviving the name given to an experimental high-performance Bentley that was destroyed by German bombs in 1939, and recalling the Cote d'Azur and the heyday of continental motoring when a car was judged on its performance between London and Monaco. The Corniche in Rolls-Royce and Bentley form is a two-door saloon or drophead with hand-built coachwork by Rolls-Royce's subsidiary company H J Mulliner, Park Ward. Although developed from the 2-door Silver Shadow/T models which it supersedes, the Corniche is considerably faster and gets its extra speed from extra power. Modifications to the V8 engine had been introduced in 1970, when emission controls had proved to be sapping the engine of its power, and the capacity was increased to 6.75-litres by way of compensation. For the Corniche the power of that engine was increased by another 10 percent, basically by

changes to the ignition and valve timing and to the breathing. The result is much better acceleration between 50 and 100mph and a maximum speed of over 120mph.

The overall styling of the Corniche is similar to that of its immediate predecessors, but there have been plenty of detailed changes in keeping with the car's more sporting character.

A redesigned facia now includes a rev counter among the instruments, and the steering wheel diameter has been reduced to 15 inches, with the steering ratio raised to 3.6 turns from lock to lock! The car now handles surprisingly well for its size, running on 205-15 radial-ply tyres as standard equipment, with improved damping and increased roll stiffness, with anti-lift geometry for the rear suspension as well as the automatic ride height control, and with an impressively compact turning circle (for this kind of car) of 38 feet.

What is more, Rolls-Royce have attempted to deal with the rust problem. Commercially available steel is

In 1971 RR revived the Corniche
name for this more powerful, more
refined and better-handling version
of the Shadow

now better than it was in the early post-war years, but still pretty rough; yet the adoption of unitary construction makes corrosion prevention absolutely vital to the safety as well as to the durability of the car. The durability of a Rolls-Royce is the foundation of its reputation, so the company has investigated the matter with some care and has standardised a thorough and comprehensive treatment.

Basically the anti-corrosion measures begin with work on the bare metal of the body shell. The structure is steel, but those areas particularly vulnerable to corrosion are made in particularly heavy-gauge steel that is zinc-coated. The doors, the bonnet and the boot lid are aluminium. All metal-to-metal contact surfaces and all spot-welded joints are painted with zinc-rich primer before assembly. Once assembly is complete, the unit goes through a ten-stage process in the paint shop at Crewe, beginning with cleaning of the body shells. Then there is a dip and spray metal cleaning and pretreatment process which chemically converts the surface of the metal into zinc phosphates. This surface coating has corrosion-inhibiting properties and gives greatly improved paint adhesion. It needs a wash off afterwards, and this is done with a distilled water spray followed by drying in the oven. Then a coat of acid etch is sprayed on by hand, and the entire body shell is totally immersed in a water-miscible primer, stored and stirred in a 7,000 gallon tank. When the body shell has been fished out and shaken off it is stoved for twenty minutes at 335°F. Then it is given a thorough inspection, its body joints are sealed with a mastic rubber, and two coats of filler are applied by hand and stoved after each coat. On top of this a coat of black paint is applied, a guide coat which aids later rubbing

The Corniche even has a revolution counter, a strange thing to find in a Rolls-Royce. Air conditioning is included in the standard specification

The new Corniche is also made as a drophead, bodied (like the Corniche saloon) by RR subsidiary Mulliner, Park Ward

down; and underneath the car no less than seventy pounds of underseal are applied.

Thereafter the body goes to the Mulliner Park Ward plant at Willesden, where it is rubbed down by hand to eliminate any irregularities before the application of another primer coat. On top of this go three double coats of colour.

At this stage, painting is suspended while the car goes out for road tests. When it comes back, the underseal is touched in and the entire under-surface

is sprayed with a thixotropic black bituminous material which forms a coat 0.015-inch thick. Finally the body paintwork is rectified and polished, involving several applications of colour coats.

Similar care is devoted to individual components. The subframes are phosphated and dip primed in the same way as the body shell, their inside surfaces being then sprayed with oil before access holes are bunged. Those pieces that are made to close tolerances are cadmium plated; those that do not have to be finished to such fine limits are enamelled black. The brake cylinder assembly and other crucial bits in vulnerable areas beneath the car are protected by shields. The exhaust sys-

tem has nickel-chromium plated mild steel pipes at the forward end and stainless steel pipes at the rear, while the silencers themselves are of stainless steel. The engine is anodised and electrolytic action between the coolant and cuprous alloys is prevented either by tinning or by nickel plating.

It is extremely impressive, and entirely worthwhile, because this is a beautiful car both in appearance and in performance. After years of producing cars which were well made but hardly modern in conception, Rolls-Royce have succeeded in designing a thoroughly good car. The motor car division manufactures other things as well as cars; small air-cooled piston engines for aircraft under licence from the Teledyne Continental Corporation of America, and other engines for commercial vehicles and the military. More to the point, it makes a profit out of its £30 million annual turnover, half of which is accounted for by cars, a third by diesels; and in 1971 that is a proud boast for any department of the company. For in the midst of events which were widely publicised, and which at the time of writing are still by no means resolved, the details published by Rolls-Royce of the new Corniche appeared beneath the scarcely credible superscript: *E R Nicholson, Receiver and Manager, appointed 4th February 1971.*

Symbol of the 20th Century

Barrie Pitt, Editor-in-Chief
Ballantine's Illustrated History Books

Few people today would doubt that the car has consolidated its place as the dominant factor in the middle years of the twentieth century.

Its influence pervades almost every aspect of life in the western world, and in the new industrial nations of the east.

Basically, this plain little machine, with an engine to propel it, brakes to slow and stop it, and a wheel to steer it, is a device for moving a small group of people from one place to another. But if that were all, there would be no call for a series such as this. The charm of the car lies in its infinite variety, in the fact that a car is an expression of almost every aspect of human life.

For a few fortunate professional drivers it provides an enjoyable way of earning a living, occasionally the opportunity to make a great deal of money. For many other thousands of young men, rally drivers, kart enthusiasts, drag racers, and amateur racing drivers, it offers a chance to extend their sporting instincts, and in some ways it may be a comparatively harmless substitute for tribal and individual warfare which modern weapons might render all too dangerous.

For others, designers and mechanics, it has provided the opportunity to try their intellectual and creative capacities to the full extent, and thousands of talented people have consequently been liberated by the challenges of automobile design from pedestrian and monotonous occupations to which they might otherwise have been condemned.

But more important than the people who make cars and drive them for sport, in terms of numbers, are the ordinary motorists who buy and use production models, and they too are of an infinite variety. It is probably true to say that in the wealthy societies of the United States and Europe, most people who want to own a car can do so, and they are thereby placed in possession of a device that immediately becomes an extension of their personalities. To some extent indeed, perhaps unjustly, people are judged according to the car they drive, and the car thus becomes a symbol of the man.

Socially, its influence is even more significant, and not entirely beneficial. It crowds our cities, making streets ugly, obstructing efficient street cleaning, destroying the fabric of buildings with its fumes, and killing people in crashes. In motion or stationary, it occupies land on a space-per-car ratio which city real estate values cannot accommodate much longer. And outside towns, roads built to carry the car carve the landscape into sections with no respect for